Living in the Light
<u>Above The Line</u>
(In a World of Turmoil)

An Invitation to Cosmic Consciousness

By
Anthony John Monaco

A Stars of the Scriptures Series

authorHOUSE™

1663 LIBERTY DRIVE, SUITE 200
BLOOMINGTON, INDIANA 47403
(800) 839-8640
WWW.AUTHORHOUSE.COM

AuthorHouse™
1663 Liberty Drive, Suite 200
Bloomington, IN 47403
www.authorhouse.com
Phone: 1-800-839-8640

AuthorHouse™ UK Ltd.
500 Avebury Boulevard
Central Milton Keynes, MK9 2BE
www.authorhouse.co.uk
Phone: 08001974150

First published by AuthorHouse 3/13/2006

ISBN: 1-4208-9481-1 (e)

ISBN: 1-4208-9480-3 (sc)

Printed in the United States of America
Bloomington, Indiana

This book is printed on acid-free paper.

Published Books of the Author

The Challenge of Moses
The Symbolic Version Of Genesis
The Symbolic Version Of Exodus
The Symbolic Version Of Job

The Mission of Jesus and John
The Symbolic Version Of The Parables Of The Master
The Symbolic Version Of John
The Symbolic Version Of Revelation

The Songs and Wisdom of David & Solomon
The Symbolic Version of Psalms
The Symbolic Version of Proverbs
The Symbolic Version Of Ecclesiastes &
The Symbolic Version Of The Song of Solomon

The Testimony of the Major Prophets
The Symbolic Version Of Isaiah
The Symbolic Version of Ezekiel
The Symbolic Version of Jeremiah &
The Symbolic Version of Lamentations
The Symbolic Version of Daniel

The Recitations of Mohammed
The Symbolic Version of the Koran

Scriptures from the Orient
The Symbolic Version of the Dhammapada
The Symbolic Version of the Tao Te Ching of Lao Tzu
The Symbolic Version of the Kitab-i-Aqdas
The Symbolic Version of the Bhagavad Gita

The Leadership of Joseph Smith
The Symbolic Version of the Book of Mormon

The Truth of Nanak and the Sikhs
The Symbolic Version of the Guru Granth Sahib Part I
The Symbolic Version of the Guru Granth Sahib Part II
The Symbolic Version of the Guru Granth Sahib Part III

The Interpretations of Anthony John Monaco
THE SPIRIT IS in the Form
Stop Dying and Start Living
Hey There! Here I Am!!
The Symbolic Version of the Wizard of Oz
(The Motion Picture)

The REAL Holy Grail

A Stars of the Scriptures Series
Living in the Light Above the Line

Copyrighted Books Of The Author

The Symbolic Version of the Guru Granth Sahib Part II
The Symbolic Version of the Guru Granth Sahib Part III
The REAL Holy Grail
(A Personal Journey into Cosmic Consciousness)

This Book is Dedicated To

MARTIN CECIL EXETER

April 27, 1909 – January 12, 1988

DR. WILLIAM H. BAHAN

September 24, 1926-July 10, 1983

Friends and Mentors
Who Shared The Light and
The Horizontal Line With Me

Table of Contents

Foreword

This book is written for any person who is interested in learning how to live peacefully in a world of turmoil, chaos and distress. There is a **WAY** for you to do this. There is a WAY of Life. It is not hard. It is very easy but it is very, very exact. In order to come to know this Way, **in your own experience,** an individual male or female must be **willing** to change. The necessary change is a movement from your present experience of turmoil, chaos and distress **before** you can experience the new Way of Life that is available to be experienced. The new state available to you is characterized by serenity, calmness, patience and understanding. This new state is available for you to dwell therein above the world of turmoil and trouble.

The troublesome state is caused by the old and familiar way in which you have viewed the world of your immediate environment; the new way is based upon a new viewpoint, a new vision, of perceiving the very same environment that surrounds you and troubles you. There are two views available to be experienced: one view is subjective, the other view is objective. The old view is varied and cloudy; the new view is exact and crystal clear. There is a "journey" of a sort involved to move from your past experience of cloudy distortion to the "new" experience of clear reality.

This journey is not a physical journey from one **ugly** physical place to another physical place of **beauty.** Many people erroneously believe, very sincerely, that they will indeed leave their personal garden of good and evil and enter, through a magic gate, into a garden of Eden. They have believed the fantasy that they can leave the mountain storms behind them and enter through a short tunnel into the beauty of Shangri La to find the place of a long and healthful life. This idea of a physical transition from ugliness to beauty is only helpful if it is used as a parable, a metaphor or an allegory, as to what really needs to occur within a person's experience

The real "journey" that needs to transpire or occur takes place in the very same place within a human body: the "journey" takes place in the <u>same space</u> occupied by the thoughts and memories of your mind as well as the feelings and emotions of your heart, your emotional realm. The real transition needs to take place in <u>your consciousness</u>. It is your consciousness that is the source of the actions that are revealed through your physical form. Your <u>consciousness</u> contains the beliefs, opinions and the facts passed down to you over many generations of time.The content of the consciousness in your particular physical body is the source of your decisions and the actions that you express into your environment. Isn't this how things really work?!

<u>LIVING IN THE LIGHT</u> Above The Line asks us to consider this simple question. "What if the content of your own consciousness, the present factual condition of your mind and heart, is not at all clear, but it is really **polluted,** and you view your environment through this pollution!? If your mind and heart are filled with pollution, impurities, false concepts and beliefs, isn't it predictable that the world of the environment that we create would be polluted and distorted, chaotic and disorderly to the very extent of the amount of pollution within us". Each of us should understand the simple concept of **Garbage In: Garbage Out**. This simple phrase applies to your present state of consciousness.

But, the problem is that there is more to your state of consciousness than simply garbage; there is also truth, creativity and beauty. The condition of your consciousness is a mixture of the garbage and the beauty. If we can represent the beauty of truth within our consciousness as crystal-clear water, and the garbage as dirt suspended in the water or dissolved in the water, then we can have a better idea of the polluted state that we bring into our specific portion of the world which we center.

We are at the center of our specific world as seen through our state of consciousness. There is no one else at the center of our world except us and we are surrounded by a state of consciousness in varying degrees of pollution depending upon our hereditary influences. Is it possible to create a clear, clean world through a polluted state of consciousness?! How can we do this!? There is a Way.

You should begin to get the picture that we live in a "polluted mind-made world" of an environment that has been created through the "polluted mass consciousness of the minds and hearts" of the inhabitants of planet Earth, past and present. We can begin to understand that the environment is a polluted mess because our messy environment has been made, and is continually being made, in our present day by a polluted state of the mass consciousness of mankind. This is a global "problem".

If you are presently observing the particular circumstances in your environment and you perceive **<u>problems</u>** instead of the predictable results of the operation of the Law of Cause and Effect to create conditions made through the consciousness of human beings who live here on Earth, then, <u>**you**</u>, not your environment, **<u>are the problem</u>**. The environment is a **<u>perfect reflection</u>** of the power of Life moving through the polluted mass consciousness to produce the polluted physical, mental and emotional forms in the material world of the environment. This is the perfect operation of the Law of Cause and Effect. This is a Law that has never been repealed. Material conditions are a perfect reproduction of the pattern in the mass consciousness.

There are many people on earth who want to change the terrible, polluted material conditions on earth by moving and changing the conditions and circumstances that have been made by the constant and consistent operation of the Law of Cause and Effect. This attempt has not worked successfully over thousands of years, has it?! The only true starting point for meaningful success is the consciousness of the **individual**. If we clean the individual consciousness, then success is absolutely assured by the operation of the Law.

You must begin with your own state of consciousness, rather than the material forms of your environment, in order to achieve the promised state of serenity and peace. Most people are self-satisfied, satisfied with the self that they know, and they want to "stay the same", to remain identified with a false state They want to use the consciousness of the false state and begin the futile attempt to "re-arrange" the world of an environment of distortion and chaos in order to achieve their goal of happiness sometime in the future. This is the **pursuit** of happiness through a polluted state of consciousness that is doomed to failure.

Most people are **unwilling** to change their concept of "This is the way I am. I've always been this way. I am satisfied with myself exactly the way I am." On this basis, there is no hope for you to achieve fulfillment because the intended future never comes through a consciousness that will not change. The goal that we present and offer to you is not an imaginary happiness in the future; it is the experience of a very real serenity and calmness in **the present**. Your goal should be serenity and peace in an understandable world of your environment.

A horizontal line has been drawn across the top of the page of a person's past experience of life, and the person who is living under this line, has no idea that there is a better way. The person is living **under** the horizontal line of separation which they themselves have drawn and which they also maintain. A person who exists underneath this line experiences a state which is characterized by a mishmash of positive and negative emotions as well as turbulent conditions which are considered to be insoluble, and never-ending problems.

People are not aware of the possibility that the horizontal line above their heads is a barrier to their growth. They don't really know that there is a place **above** the line. People can and should live **above** the line where they can see their environments, circumstances and situations objectively and exactly as they are. The place **above** the line is an unknown place <u>in your consciousness</u> which is only one step away from the familiar and known place in consciousness which is **below** the line.

The author offers a new vision which is available from an observation point at a higher level in consciousness which is only one step away, one step to a place that is above the line. The resultant clarity of vision will provide a course of constructive action that is not available when the person remains below the line..

In my previous books of the **Stars of the Scriptures Series**, I have referred to ***LIVING IN THE LIGHT Above The Line*** in scriptural or religious terms: such as, the Promised Land of Moses, the Kingdom of Heaven of Jesus, the Nirvana of the Buddha, the Divine Radiance of the Shekinah of the Old Testament, Unity Consciousness, Cosmic Consciousness, Christ Consciousness, and the Oneness with Source.

In this book, I have purposely stayed away from over-emphasis on scripture and religious texts in favor of the more provable scientific method. The ultimate goal is the same: Proving to your Self Who you really are and what **YOU** are doing on earth so that you can fulfill your mission.

It is the author's purpose in this book to lead the willing and interested reader, as simply and as accurately as possible, to the path of the way to ***LIVING IN THE LIGHT Above The Line*** to experience *Cosmic Consciousness*.

Chapter I:
There Is a Land Above The Line -
(In a World of Turmoil.)

The Land Above The Line

I have drawn a horizontal, solid, black line across the top of this page. It may seem to you that there is nothing **above** the solid black line---except empty space. Blankness. A void. Caution! It only **appears** that the space above the line is blank. The purpose of this book is to acquaint you with the land above the line so that you can live there.

The solid black line and the written words **under** the line are **visible**; the **space above** the visible, black line is presently **invisible** to you. The words under the line are visible and they represent **the forms** of the material things. The space above the line is invisible and this invisible space represents the invisible spirit of Life that is available in your consciousness and the heretofore invisible designs of the forms of life which are only a potential that are available to actualized. There is a place above the line.

The title of this book is ***LIVING IN THE LIGHT Above The Line.*** **It could also be called Consistent LIVING in the <u>space</u> that exists <u>above the line</u>. It could also be called living in the spirit**

of Life. The fact that something is invisible does not mean that it doesn't exist. Air is invisible to the human eye, but it exists. Life is invisible--but it exists even though we can't see it with our ordinary physical senses. In fact, we would die without air to breathe. Also, we would be classified as "dead" if we did not have Life present in our human forms. If you have ever visited the body, the remains, of a former friend in a funeral home, you should have been aware, due to the absence of breathing air and the cold temperature of the corpse, that there was no life present in that form.

An invisible spirit of Life exists above the line in each person who is alive. If we are interested in ***LIVING IN THE LIGHT Above The Line***, the invisible substance of the Spirit of LIFE is the necessary, basic requirement for LIVING. The nature of life is to be Alive. Life lives! "Dead" life, whatever Life is, would be a contradiction in terms. It is life's nature to be alive. If life is not present, "we", if we identify only with the physical form, are dead. But the fact is that we are not dead. If you are reading this paragraph in this moment, you know that you are not a corpse. YOU are alive in a human form. This is the simplest indicator and proof that Life is present.

Since ***LIVING IN THE LIGHT Above The Line*** requires an atmosphere of Life to be present above the line, then it is a requirement of life to allow real living to transpire above the line. If the Spirit of Life is present **above the line**, then, the people who are searching for invisible Life can never find it while they are **below** the line in the measurable, material forms of things. People are aware that all living forms of Life, that are both alive and well, have life moving through their forms of atoms and molecules.

Perhaps you, the reader, can begin to sense that our journey from below the line to the invisible space above the line is a journey from the visible forms of things to the invisible essence of the life of things that exists and is available to be experienced above the line. The forms of things without the essence of life are dead things. Dead things break and decay because they have no Life within them. Dead things are characterized by the **evidence of the absence of life**. Living things are characterized by **evidence of the presence**

2

of life <u>within</u> the physical forms. We should be interested in the presence and the location of the Reality of Life.

Life is vitally important because when life is present **within the forms**, the material things are alive and they thrive and they grow! When Life is absent from within the physical forms of things, then decay and disintegrative change occurs.The act of LIVING requires the movement of Life within the forms in general, and the movement of Life in human forms in particular. It is wise to assume that the Reality of Life is present in our human form as long as we are alive.

In order to experience Life more abundantly, the human form must allow the flow and movement of Life through the human form. The human form is composed of a physical **body**, a consciousness of the physical body (which we call the **mind**), and the emotional nature of the physical body, (which we call the **heart** of one's emotions.)In short, the human form contains the physical component, the mental component, the emotional component, and **LIFE. In most discussions, Life is omitted from consideration.**

Let me repeat. It is the nature of Life to be alive and to live. It's nature is to be alive. The spirit of LIFE is permanent. "Dead" LIFE is a contradiction in terms. If life could die, it wouldn't be Life. However, the physical form, with its mind and heart, are subject to constant change from the moment of conception onward. The physical human form has a limited and temporary existence in space and time while we are on earth in a human form until Life separates from the human form. Life's nature is to be alive. The real treasure is Life, not form. Why do we make this distinction between Life and form?!

It is possible for the human consciousness to rise up from identification with the physical form of the human body and its material environment to experience the Life that is Above the Line. It is to this journey upward from the human consciousness that you know to a higher level of consciousness, Cosmic Consciousness, to which you have been invited. Human consciousness has been conditioned over many centuries to believe that there is either

nothing after death, or that there is **Something** within the human form that survives. Which is the Truth? Can it be proven!?

The human consciousness has been programmed to believe that the requirement for entrance to this place of survival is the **death** of the human form. "Yes, you have to die to get there!" But people innately know that they don't want to leave the Earth and **die** to get **there**, they want to Live and to experience the eternal nature of Life while they are still **here**. People want to experience Life and they want to experience it more abundantly. People sense and know that there is some semblance of Life on Earth because they are alive and they are here.

Could it be possible that we have been living in a lower state, symbolized by our experience of living **below** the horizontal line that has been drawn on earth, while there is a higher state of ***LIVING IN THE LIGHT Above The Line*** that has always been available to be experienced by those who are willing to use their freedom of choice to go on a remarkable journey?! You are being invited to go on this remarkable journey!

This Land Above the Line is available to you. There is a Path, a Way, to rise up in consciousness to a new and higher level that has been beyond the awareness of what we have known as "human nature" and "We are only human, you know!" It is a Higher Nature than we have ever known. This Higher Nature is governed by the Law of Life.

What we are labeling as a Higher Nature is not really "Higher". It only **seems** higher because we have been functioning at a **lower** level for generations. Actually, this Higher Nature is our True Nature. What we have called "human nature" is a lower form of our True Nature which is available to be experienced as we begin ***LIVING IN THE LIGHT Above The Line***. We must be willing to ascend the levels of consciousness to experience our True Nature. As we begin our journey upward into unknown and unfamiliar territory, we should be prepared to leave the pollution, the pollution in our consciousness, behind.

Nothing of value will be lost as we leave the familiar area below the line and begin our journey upward to the land of ***LIVING IN THE LIGHT Above The Line***, which is on **this side of the grave**. You should be pleased to hear that our destination is on this side of the grave and that you don't have to die to get to the land above the line.

You should also be aware that there is One Law in Operation during your journey upward. You have had some experience of the **successful harmonization** of the operation of this Law in your past experience; and you have also had some experience of **resisting** the Law in the **futile and painful attempt to get what you wanted** in your human nature experience. It is much easier to harmonize with the operation of the Law of Life. Be prepared to leave the emotionally painful experiences behind you.

Let us look at this Law in more detail. If you desire to continue on our journey to the land above the line, you **MUST** know the LAW. You **MUST** also obey the LAW. You MUST also accept the conditions made by the operation of the LAW. It is emotionally painful for you to resist the operation of the LAW.

Chapter 2: There Is A Law Of Life

Life operates on land, in the oceans, in the air and in the observable universe according to certain laws. Scientifically, certain of these laws have been identified in the sciences that we know as physics, chemistry, biology, astronomy, etc. The evidence of life in action through living creatures is seen everywhere in the seas, on the land and in the air. When Life is not moving through the forms of things, we say that the forms are dead. They have no life moving through them any more.

Every material thing on Earth can be called a **thing of Life**. Religionists call the presence of Life on Earth an aspect of God. Some scientists will admit that the theory of evolution requires the presence of Life, whatever Life is, to bring about the forms necessary for the evolutionary process to transpire over millions of years. Life is present in all the forms of evolution. Other scientists state that the evolutionary changes occur simply by undirected chance. They believe that forms of Life just happened for no reason even though the forms of life are beautifully constructed and demonstrate an intelligent design.

As human beings, with Life moving through us, (we are alive, after all), we find ourselves observing other forms of human beings, as well as the forms of life in the oceans, on the land and in the air. We possess the intelligence to study and to classify all of the forms of life on earth into an intelligent data base of information. We have come a long way from our "caveman" days.

We have filled encyclopedias with the knowledge that we have gained.There seems to be an intelligent design to the material things of the world that we have studied. There seems to be laws at work, and these laws operate in predictable patterns. We can trust these laws of physics, chemistry, biology and astronomy to predict very accurately the way that changes will occur in these material forms in the world of matter.

Human beings are classified by some scientists as members of the **animal** kingdom. Others, particularly religious leaders, put human beings in a separate category, called the **Kingdom of Man**. There is no question that Man has both a potential and a performance far above the animal, vegetable and mineral kingdoms. Human beings also have the potential to destroy ourselves and the other "lower" kingdoms of the Earth by our decisions and our behaviors. We have observed over the millennia of recorded history that mankind, in general, has the ability to be very creative and very destructive. Life moving through human beings who comprise the body of mankind has the ability to be creative or destructive.

In fact, each individual within the body of mankind, male or female, has this ability to be either creative or destructive **in each and every moment that we are alive**, as long as Life is moving through us. We have the freedom to choose whether our actions shall be creative or destructive. Life, or evolution, has given us this ability to choose. We have the ability to think and to feel and to exhibit a behavior that directly affects the world in which we live. This ability **to choose our individual behavior** is a law of life on planet Earth. We have the ability to choose what we express, the nature of our expression. You may be getting the idea that we are going to **choose** to be creative rather than destructive on our journey.

Life has also given to us the intelligent understanding that whatever we express through our hearts, minds and bodies shall appear in our environment as forms. Our feelings, our thoughts, our desires that are released into the environment shall appear on earth in observable forms. We can observe the results of our expressions. We can see the Law of Cause and Effect in operation through the consciousness of mankind to produce the material conditions in the environment. Mankind creates the conditions on earth in which we must live. Whatever conditions we make in our consciousness, we must live in these conditions as the appear in material form. The Theory of Evolution did not create a skyscraper. Our large buildings were made of materials through a design that appeared in human consciousness and then we built it, created it, in our material world.

Each of us is a member of the body of mankind as long as we have life moving through the human capacities which are under our direct control. We have lived long enough to know that Life does not tell us what to do. In fact, in our own experience, we know personally that the Law of Cause and Effect is in operation. We know, personally, that "As We Sow, So Shall We Reap". This is not a religious belief, it is a true statement of the way things work as we function within the Law of Cause and Effect, the One Law that is never repealed.

People have "prayed", uttered magic words, participated in strange offerings, promised change in personal behaviors, vowed to give up their sins, if only the Law of Life, the Law of Cause and Effect might be changed for "them". Fortunately, Life's Law of Cause and Effect has never been repealed to suit an individual's personal desires, prayers, greed or wants. Life just keeps flowing through Life's creations to produce conditions according to the operation of the Law.

The stability of this Law is a wonderful thing. Since the Law does not change based upon the various whims of individuals, we can always count upon the Law of Cause and Effect to work **<u>ALWAYS</u>**! I have never seen one example of any instance where the Law of Cause and Effect has ever failed to function. There have been claims that the Law did not work but the claim has not been demonstrated or repeated.

Perhaps mankind has "evolved" to the point in our evolution that, for our own sake and our own survival, we can begin to work with the Certainty of the Unchangeable Law of Life. Instead of choosing **destructive** thoughts, feelings and behaviors, we can choose **creative** thoughts, feelings and behaviors. We do have freedom of choice, the freedom to choose, in any circumstance if we choose to use it. Never forget this. Creative choices produce creative results, **Always**. Destructive choices produce destructive results, **Always**. The rules of life are really simple, aren't they?!

We can be either Creative or Destructive with the assurance and the absolute certainty that the Law will continue to function and never be repealed. We reap what we sow.As we become aware of this, let us begin to change the nature of our sowing in our consciousness if we really want to change the nature of the forms of the environmental world in which we live. The Law will not fail to operate. You can count on it, 100%

Now, observe the world in which we find ourselves. We the people who live on planet Earth created this **turmoil and chaos** in the land below the line through our collective consciousness by our **choices** and the predictable results of the consistent operation of the Law of Cause and Effect. The Law will not change. However, our **behaviors** can change, **if we choose**, as we learn to live above the line where turmoil and chaos are absent.

Here are the ingredients for the terrible
conditions in the land below the line:
The Law. People. Consciousness. Choices.Results.
Did you notice that people have made some <u>wrong choices, and
right choices,</u> to produce the conditions of the
land of turmoil and chaos!?
Are you getting the idea that we are going to learn and to
choose how to make right choices!?

Chapter 3: There is a Land of Turmoil and Chaos

There is a land of turmoil and chaos.It is a very familiar place to us. It is the environmental world in which we live. It is a world that has been built through our choices. It is symbolized as the land **Below** the Horizontal Line. People who are positioned to live in the land below the line do not really have the **full** experience of Life. They have an experience of existing in a global environment which is characterized by the many "problems of the world". It is the familiar land that we have inherited from our great grandfathers, grandfathers and fathers who passed these distorted conditions down through the generations of time to us. The Law worked! We should observe the conditions in the world and know the choices that they made to produce these conditions.

We have been programmed by our inheritance from the past and we have followed the customs of old by contributing our personal share to the patterns of distortion, turmoil and chaos in the present. As we plant the seeds of our distorted inheritance from the past and our own contributions to the environment in the present, why would we ever expect our future to be anything other than **more of the same**. The Law of Cause and Effect is never repealed! We will reap what we sow and that is a fair and just law. The answer for a better future will not be found in a continuation of what we have been doing for millennia. What can one person do!?

We have seen that our individual contribution to the environment is created as Life moves through our specific state of consciousness, as Life moves through the content of our individual heart and mind, through our individual body to create the conditions of the harvest field of our environment. This is the Way that the Law of Life works on earth through a person. Our individual consciousness is only a very small part of the mass consciousness of mankind. But, it's all that **we** have!

This simple fact was demonstrated to me as I sat in a large stadium at a college football game where I was one person among 40,000 spectators who composed a sea of people. I became aware that my individual consciousness was like a thimbleful of liquid consciousness in an entire ocean of liquid and changing consciousness. I was also aware that Life was moving **simultaneously** through the consciousness of not only every person in the stadium, but also through the billions of people on earth in each and every moment of time.

It was not hard to realize that I had no control over the process of Life moving through the thousands and billions of thimblefuls of "liquid consciousness" in the minds and hearts of the sea of all people as the conditions on Earth are given form in the total environment. It was easy to realize that the **only valid starting point** for any real, meaningful change for the world was what was expressed through my individual thimbleful of consciousness. A single thimbleful of consciousness is not very much to work on when compared to the entire sea of mass consciousness.

As one individual, a single thimbleful of consciousness was a manageable amount of the total problems of the world for me to handle. My responsibility was to work on my thimbleful of consciousness and leave the rest of the world alone to handle their thimblefuls. I could comprehend clearly for the first time in my life why we the people cannot ever solve "all the problems in the material world at once", which is the quick solution that most people want to see.

 Life doesn't work that way. The Law doesn't work that way either. The answer comes in thimblefuls of consciousness that add up to the total consciousness of mankind. I have absolutely no control over the thimbleful of consciousness in the mind of another person. Every person has potential control of their own thimbleful. Life designed us that way.

I could see that the problems in the environment do not originate in **the forms** of the material world of the environment; **the problems originate in the thimblefuls of liquid consciousness** which are filled with customs, opinions, beliefs, etc. in our individual minds and hearts that we have inherited from the past.We add our little bit of **pollution** or **clarity** in this present generation through our thimbleful of consciousness. This creative process has been going on for generations. If we add our bit of pollution in the present, it is an evil generation. If we add some clear and clean behavior, then that is what we generate and create. Simple and clear.

This creative process is multiplied by billions of people on earth who do not know the impact of what they are doing to the whole through their thimbleful of consciousness. The conditions of the world very accurately reflect the state of consciousness that exists within people. Globally, our world conditions are made by the totality of us. **This is the operation of the Law that will not change.** We must accept the way things really work because this is the way that Life works on earth through people. The Law won't change.

The conditions that we observe on earth are the outworking of this process: Life moves through consciousness to create conditions in the world. The physical forms, the mental forms, the emotional forms are the **perfect reflection** of the patterns or designs that are contained in the mass consciousness based upon the operation of the Law of Sowing and Reaping. The only beginning for meaningful change is through one's personal consciousness. We must work with what is in our particular thimbleful of consciousness and let Life shine through it. Wait a minute! Not so fast!

Our thimbleful of consciousness is filled with the **POLLUTED STUFF** that created the distorted conditions of turmoil and chaos in the land BELOW the line where we live and which we created in our ignorance. As long as our polluted state of consciousness remains in our minds and hearts, we will constantly re-create the polluted Land of turmoil and chaos. Almost everyone is contributing to the re-creation of these distorted conditions and circumstances of the world. Is there any way in which we can learn and know how the world of beauty, that everyone would like to see on earth, can come into manifestation as Life moves through us? That would be wonderful knowledge!

We need to take a closer look at what is contained in the mass consciousness, which contains our thimbleful, that produces the conditions that exist in the Land Below the Line, which is our present world environment filled with turmoil and chaos.

The "liquid" ocean of polluted mass consciousness contains the **feelings** and the **thoughts** of everything that eventually appears on earth in various forms on earth. Mass consciousness is filled with both creative and destructive **thoughts** that appear on earth in creative or destructive patterns. People really know whether their expressed actions are helpful or harmful to the global society. People know immediately with their conscious minds what they express creatively or destructively at the moment of expression. You **know** what you express at the very moment of expression.

The only point of real control occurs BEFORE the action is expressed into the world through the human equipment. Once the action is released from one's consciousness, it can never be pushed back. Expression is a one way street that must be played out in the environment. If you give birth to it, if you let it out, then **WE** have to live with it. Are you getting the idea that **creative** thoughts expressed from your thimbleful of consciousness should be moved from below the Line to **ABOVE** the Line. Good!

The mass consciousness Below the Line is filled with mixed emotions. We are aware by personal observation, newspapers, radio, television, gossip, etc of the **negative** emotions in people that produce murder, jealousy, anger, blame, greed, thievery, arson, addiction, anxiety, road rage, impatience, unkindness, fear, etc. These negative emotions do not feel "good" when they are expressed from us. They are unpleasant feelings.

The religions call the actions from these negative emotions, **Sins**. The word, Sin, comes from an old Anglo-Saxon term used in archery. Sin, simply means that the arrow that has left the bow is "off-the mark", off the target. If the arrow hits the target or the bulls-eye, it is called, "In". A **sin** is a negative emotion or feeling. An **in** is a positive emotion or feeling. Are you getting the idea that an **In** should be moved above the line, and the **Sin** should remain below the line? Good.

There are **positive** emotions in the mass consciousness that produce different behaviors. These emotions feel "good" and they are desirable experiences when they are expressed through a physical body.. These emotions are given names like love, kindness, patience, understanding, appreciation, helpfulness, courage, thankfulness, etc. The actions from these positive emotions are called **virtues**. Each of us has virtues.

In the Land Below the Line, the movement of Life through human consciousness that contains the mixture of both the positive and negative emotions produces the distorted conditions of turmoil and chaos that coexist along with the beautiful conditions of harmony and order. The movement of Life **always** makes conditions from designs in the consciousness as it moves through the heart, mind and physical body. The Law works! The conditions on earth are now understandable on this basis. Environmental conditions can be no other way based upon what is contained in human consciousness.

Are you getting the idea that the positive emotions that create beauty and order should be included in the Land **ABOVE** the Line!? Good.

Are you getting the idea that negative emotions that create turmoil and chaos should be left in the Land **Below** the Line!? Good.

Are you beginning to understand the logic as to why the conditions in the environmental world are **exactly** the material reflection of what is expressed through the mass consciousness? Good.

Can you begin to see that conditions that have already been made can be **no other way** than the material patterns made from the design in consciousness? The Law worked to produce these conditions. The Law will not change! The conditions can be no other way once they have been expressed from consciousness. This path is a one-way street that is protected by the Law of Sowing and Reaping, the Law of Cause and Effect. What we observe of the conditions in the land below the line are **exactly** what should be there. Why call these predictable creations, "problems". The conditions can be no other way. What was made is the correct result and can be no other way. The Law made the conditions. Isn't that fair and just?!

There is a tendency to think that the expression from one's consciousness, creative or destructive, is almost automatic and, due to the speed of the action, that **it can't be helped**. It may seem that we have little or no control. We have been programmed by family, friends and peers into negative and destructive patterns of behavior without thinking about the consequences of our actions. We have reaped what we sowed!

There is a tendency to feel that the expression of emotions from one's consciousness, positive or negative, is almost automatic and, due to the speed of our emotional expression, that the emotional outbursts can't be controlled. We have a tendency to take credit for our positive expressions that are our virtues. We also have a tendency to blame our negative outbursts as "just the way we were made" as we were conditioned by family, friends, enemies and peers. We just can't help ourselves. But we have freedom to choose.

These thoughts of lack of control from our negative behaviors are the evidence a **denial** of our freedom of choice, and also a **resistance**

to change our past behaviors that have created the land below the line. This is a lack of desire and willingness to change and to live **ABOVE** the Line. Do not buy into these thoughts and feelings of failure. You do have Freedom of Choice. You do have the potential to choose what you will express through your heart, your mind and your body into your world.

The impulse of Life is moving through you, in a creative and an upward direction, to aid you to sense and to see what it is like to live **above the line** for short periods of time. There is a parable of a jumping mouse who has the ability to jump very high above the clouds for a short moment where the sun is always shining to get a quick glimpse of an orderly, beautiful and glorious state----- before the law of gravity pulled him back to earth into his world as a mouse.

Many people can identify with the Parable of the Jumping Mouse in their own experience. We have all jumped up from our state below the line to get a temporary glimpse of the land above the line before crashing down to earth to the familiar habitat of the mouse. All of us have had some experience of the higher view before we returned to "the familiar earth where we think that we belong". If this is your experience, you have identified with being a mouse!

Look in the mirror! You are not a mouse. You are Thinking Man, male or female, made in the image and likeness of something much higher than a mouse. Man, mankind, was designed to live **Above the Line**. The answer for man is not in the view of the Jumping Mouse with its short glimpse of the beauty of things. The answer for Man is to Live Above the Line. If you choose, you can learn to **Live ABOVE the Line** consistently. But you must choose. And you do have freedom of choice.

Chapter 4: You Have the Freedom to Choose.

Life is always in motion, constantly flowing through all living forms, including human forms. Life is moving through all human beings who are alive, **simultaneously**. Life is moving through your individual human consciousness that contains both the positive emotions and the negative emotions to produce conditions and circumstances in the world of your environment. Every living human being on earth is experiencing this very same process that you are in this very moment.Can you sense that something universal is at work?!

The invisible flow of Life through everyone can be called the spirit of Life as it moves through you and it is a powerful. force as it moves simultaneously through the human, animal, vegetable and mineral kingdoms of the earth. We have seen examples of the power of life in action as we observe a blade of grass forcing its way through the asphalt or concrete as it is moving toward the light of day to continue its growth.The power of Life is available to lift all of us Above the line if we choose to "go with the direction of the flow" and harmonize with the moving power of Life. Life has direction as well as power. Life is moving through your human form in varying degrees of intensity.

Human beings have power. We have the power of Life and we have the power to choose what we will do with the power that flows continuously without ceasing through our hearts, minds and bodies. Life gives us the power and the freedom to choose what we will create with the gift of life force that is flowing through us. We have the ability to create while we are alive in our earthly forms. We can create beauty and order, or we can create turmoil and chaosThe choice is ours.

It is very easy to observe the world which we have created as life moved through our consciousness. Look at the conditions and circumstances that we have created! The conditions on earth very accurately and precisely reveal what we have chosen to create in our consciousness, in our minds and hearts, and subsequently released into the world of our environment. The Law works and reflects our choices, Always!

We created these present conditions by the totality of our individual behaviors. This is the operation of the Law of Life based upon our choices, individually and collectively. The Law of Cause and Effect never ceases and it always works. As we sow our choices, we reap our choices. This is a very fair and logical system that Life has produced on Earth. Are you getting the idea that Life, whatever it is, might be intelligent!?

We, the inhabitants of planet Earth over many generations, created the conditions on earth, and we must live in the conditions which we created. Mankind has chosen to call itself, ***Homo Sapiens***, thinking man, man who thinks. We can either think and understand the operation of the Law and harmonize with the Law to create order and beauty, or we can use our freedom of choice to ignore the precise operation of the Law.

We can remain selfish and self-centered and do whatever we feel like doing to make us "happy" and hope for good results in the world. Look at what we've done! We have created turmoil, chaos, disorder, famine, pestilence, greed and death. Man is not a living soul, mankind is a sick and a dying soul. The conditions of the

18

world below the line call out to us that we have a problem. The problem is global in nature.

As we refuse to change the nature of our behavior, our sowing, we absolutely shall continue, over many generations of time, to repeat the same mistakes that were made by our forefathers. As we continue to ignore the Law of Life that will never change, we shall continue to create the same distorted conditions about which we so loudly complain. Why should we complain if these are the **exact** conditions that we have made? If we immediately stop complaining about our world, we will immediately begin to move toward ***LIVING IN THE LIGHT Above The Line*** because there is really nothing to complain about in our world. We created it, didn't we!? We should take responsibility for our creation and not call our creations, "Problems".

We have learned to call these conditions that are unsatisfactory to us by an acceptable name: we call them **Problems**. In our stupidity, we continue to ignore the Law of Life, the Law of Cause and Effect, and we use our freedom of choice in a new, misdirected effort of spending our time, and hard work in a futile attempt to solve these problems, which are not problems. We try to change the problems that we created into **Answers or Solutions**. This is as impossible as trying to turn stones into bread.

Problems that originated in the consciousness of man, which are below the Line, are given physical form in the world of atoms and molecules by the operation of the Law. The molecular arrangements of things created are exactly the way that they were created to be. **They can be no other way**. The problems, so called, are a perfect material replica of the design that was created in consciousness. This is the way things work and it will not change. **Isn't that scientific!?**

Everything that is on earth in material forms is exactly the way that they were created in the mind-made world. The mind-made world of people who live below the line ignored the accuracy of the Law of Cause and Effect, the Law of Life and Life itself. If anything needs to be changed in our mixed up world of turmoil and chaos, it is our thimbleful of consciousness. The mind and hearts, the polluted consciousness that exists in people who live below the Line, is not the clear consciousness that exists **Above the Line**. Clear answers do not derive from a polluted source. We need to learn to see the forms on earth exactly as they are. Conditions and circumstances **as they are** provide the raw materials and the starting point for the creative actions of people who are ***LIVING IN THE LIGHT Above The Line.*** We can use our freedom of choice to depart the land of the polluted state and rise up to the land of ***LIVING IN THE LIGHT Above The Line***. In our upward journey, we can deliberately choose to leave the pollution of the negative emotions behind us as unnecessary baggage that will only weigh us down. This journey is easy and the burden is light. We are on our Way as our consciousness is rising to a new level.

Chapter 5: Everything Observed Has Already Occurred

Here is some Good News! As we continue to observe the land of turmoil and chaos in which we live, you should begin to be aware of the fact that the more clearly you see the actual condition of the distortions of the world in which we live, and how these conditions were made, then you are automatically ascending, **rising up**, toward the Land Above the Line. You are on an upward Path.

The more clearly that you see the present conditions of the world in which we live, the **higher** you are on the mountain of increased perception. It is good to see things clearly, exactly the real way that they are in the material world and not the imaginary way that you would like them to be. As you objectively view the conditions of the world and know that they can be no other way than the way they are, you are on the ascending path.

The land below the line is the **polluted mind-made world** into which we have been born. It is filled with both creative and destructive thoughts of the mind as well as all the positive and negative emotions of the heart which were used to create the material forms in the environment. The true design and beauty of Life that would naturally and easily appear through a **clear** consciousness is presented to the environment, but the inherent order and beauty has been distorted by the **cloudy** pollution that exists in our inherited state of consciousness of the people. Present conditions can be no other way on this basis. You should understand this.

A **distorted** design is evidence of the **potential** presence of a **true design**. The present distorted design is the evidence of the **absence** of the true design. The distorted design that we observe in our material world has already been created in material forms from the pollution that exists in consciousness. Remember the creative process: Life moves through consciousness to create conditions. The Law always works.

We should begin to see clearly that the conditions on earth that we observe have already been made by the creative process. New material conditions are being made in each and every moment as the current of Life moves through the mass consciousness of the people on earth. Everything that we observe has already been made by the operation of the Law through human consciousness to produce the material conditions that we observe.

As we see and understand this process, we are beginning to see **objectively**, the way things really are, rather than **subjectively,** the **"nice"** way that we would like them to be. If we see the world subjectively, the way that we would like the world to be to please us, then we are emotionally upset about the conditions of the world. We actually insert more distortions of the true design through our negative emotions from our upset state.

Our perception of things in the material world is in the <u>process of change</u>. We begin to see more vividly. Our perception, our vision, is changing from night, to dusk, to dawn toward mid-day when the sun is at its highest and there are no shadows. The change that is transpiring is not in the material objects in the environment at which we are intently gazing. The atoms and molecules at which we are looking remain the same: but, the way that we **perceive** the material things of the environment is what is undergoing a change. Our perception is changing. We are gaining new vision, a clearer vision.

The condition of our consciousness, like viewing through various gradations of polluted water, is changing from muddy, to the cloudiness of coarse and then fine suspended particles, to opaqueness, to clear as crystal. Can you make the association of change from destructive to creative thoughts in your own **mind**!? Can you make the association of change from the negative to the positive emotions in your own **heart**? Can you be honest enough to admit that your thoughts and your emotions are in your own mind and your own heart? Will you begin to accept responsibility for your thoughts and feelings!? Are you willing to let your view of things change from what you would like to see to what is really there to be seen!?

People who dwell in the land below the line sincerely, but incorrectly, believe that their thoughts and feelings are made by the **activities in the environment**. Something happens in the world which makes them think vindictive thoughts and they feel terrible, negative emotions in their hearts which they use as an excuse to proceed to take "remedial" action, **to get even for the hurt that they feel**, to fight back. As long as a person lives below the line, and refuses to change, they will never learn how things really work and they will never rise above the turmoil and the chaos.

It takes some honesty for a person to realize that the thoughts in one's mind are one's own thoughts. It takes honesty for people to admit that all of their emotions are one's own feelings--**100%**. Your thoughts and your emotions are in your own consciousness. If you have negative feelings of anger, resentment, jealousy, envy, greed, hate, apathy, etc., these feelings are in your consciousness. They must be within you in order for you to **feel** them. The source of your feelings are **not** from the material world. They are stored in your subconscious mind.

If something occurs in your environment that comes to your consciousness as waves of sound for your ears, pictures for your eyes, taste, touch, or odors, the vibrations from the environment trigger thoughts and the negative emotions which already exist in your consciousness. As we become aware of the negative feeling in our conscious mind, we then blame the other person or condition for "making" the anger that has been stored in our subconscious mind all along and the feeling of anger is released from there.

If we continue to blame someone or something <u>external</u> to us for something that exists <u>internal</u> to us, then we will never get rid of our anger pattern. The same reasoning applies to hatred, resentment, jealousy, selfishness, greed, fear, sadness, depression, distress, etc. that we have stored up inside us. Our feelings are ours. They are an inside job.

If we accept responsibility and ownership for ALL of our negative emotions, then we are in position to cast them out of our hearts when we become aware of their presence. This is sending your heart to the laundry to wash the dirt away from a polluted and impure heart. We have no need to hold on to the dirt if we desire a clean dwelling place. We can never abide in a clean dwelling place if we don't clean house of our negative emotions.

As our heart is cleansed in the flow of Life, our heavy emotional load is lightened. How can we have an untroubled heart if we do not let go of the negative emotions which are the source of the trouble? Negative emotions are a heavy burden to carry through your experience of Life on Earth. Let go of the heavy load.

As long as people believe that someone **outside** of oneself is capable of making the negative emotions which are an "inside job", that person will never participate in the process of cleansing the heart. That person will remain a puppet to the strings pulled by other people and things in the environment. As long as a person thinks that someone else is causing his or her negative emotions, they will blame the other person and demand that that individual "take back" the negative emotion which only exists **within** the person who is experiencing the negative emotion.

Everything that occurs in the environment has already happened **before** your conscious mind and heart are aware of the external action. Did you remember that all forms in the material world were created from a pattern or design that began in human consciousness?It is necessary for any external event to have taken place in the environment **before** you are aware of the thoughts and the feelings that are triggered by the external action on your mind and heart. As long as the heart is not cleansed, we cannot see our environments clearly and achieve the mastery which results from ***LIVING IN THE LIGHT Above The Line***.

The reason is simple. We see our world through our emotional realm, our hearts, and we are aware of the conditions in our world through our conscious minds. We have to learn to use our polluted hearts and our minds correctly.

Chapter 6: The Disagreement Between Your Heart with Your Mind

During the previous chapter, we should have become aware of the need for the heart of your emotional realm to become cleansed because as long as your heart is not clean, you cannot see your environment clearly through the pollution of the negative emotions. Life needs a clean heart for your mind to see clearly through your individual human form. It should be obvious that a clear and clean consciousness of the individual mind and the heart is a **mandatory** **requirement** for an individual person to see his or her environment exactly as it is. The material world, in any given moment, is exactly what it is as createdby the Law. The challenge is to see it clearly.

There are only 5 factors at work in every person on earth. There is the presence of **Life**, the **heart,** the **mind**, the **physical body** and the **things in the environment which are made of molecules** that need to be seen exactly as they are. The molecular composition of the objects in the environment can **NEVER** be wrong. The objects are what they are even though the mind does not see the objects clearly and the heart does not want to accept, emotionally, what the mind is presenting to the heart for consideration. The material objects in the environment must be accepted as the correct starting point for clear vision.

It is true that **12** different people can view **one** incident and they can come up with 12 different interpretations of <u>exactly the same event</u>, but the differences are always in the consciousness of the12 observers who differ with each other. The differences are always in the minds and the hearts of the observers and never in the object being observed. There was only one incident and, if there were a video record of the actual incident, the pictorial record can never be incorrect if the objective camera captured the scene accurately.

It is necessary for the conscious mind to come into exact agreement with the pattern in the environment (it's like taking a picture!) because the arrangement of the materials are exactly what they should be according to the operation of the Law of Cause and Effect. It is logical and reasonable for the mind to come into agreement with the way things are in the environment because the incidents or objects in the environment in any given moment are no other way than the way they were created according to the Law.

Your conscious mind does not contain the <u>actual</u> material objects from the environment. The mind contains only **<u>images</u>** of the actual things that are observed. The material objects always remain in the environment. If there is an **incorrect image** in the mind, it is possible that the person needs corrective eyeglasses or hearing aids. **It is also possible that there is an inner distortion of the image observed that is caused by a polluted heart**.

We should remember that the conscious mind deals with intelligence and logic; the heart, the emotional realm, deals with feelings and emotions. The mind and the heart within an individual are not always in agreement with each other even though, ideally, they should be in agreement with each other because they both are in the same physical body and observing only **one** external object.

While we are on earth in a physical body, we know that we have a mind and a heart to process our thoughts and our feelings. These three capacities on earth can be symbolized by an equilateral triangle--each side of the triangle represents a body, a mind and the heart, or emotional realm.The three sides enclose an "invisible" empty space which symbolizes the invisible nature of Life that touches all three sides from within the triangle. We know that Life is present because we are alive. If Life is not present, the body, mind and heart no longer work.

Consider this example that can be used as an analogy. We can **not** be a car and the driver of the car at the same time. We are either the **driver** of the car or the **equipment**. We cannot be both the operator of the car and the equipment of the car that we are using at the same time. We are One or the other. We are the Operator of the car. The car cannot drive itself without an Operator. Let us apply this analogy to the equipment of our heart, our mind and our body.

We know that we have a heart because we are alive and we have feelings. We know that we have the ability to **use** our feelings and that we can **change** our feelings. If we can change our feelings, we are not our feelings. We are the **One** who changed them.

We know that we have a mind because we are alive and we can think. We know that we are not our mind and our thoughts because we have the ability to **use our mind, change our mind** and **change** our thoughts. We are the **One** who changes our mind and our thoughts.

We know that we have the equipment of a physical body.We can **use** our body, we can **move** our body, touch it and see our reflection of it. We are the **One** who moves our body as we choose.The One we are has the ability to change our feelings, change our mind, our thoughts and manipulate the equipment of our body. The **One** that we are has this power. It is the power that is **greater** and **higher** than the equipment of our body, mind and heart if we choose to use this power. WE can identify with Being inside the triangle.

We are aware that Life is moving through the heart, the mind and the physical body and we are aware that we are in an earthly environment. There should be understanding that Life is in the human form with a heart and a mind that finds itself at a specific place on planet Earth in this very moment. We are aware of time and place. **We are alive on planet Earth in this very moment and in this place!**

If there is a problem, it is not that we do not have Life. It is not that we are not on planet Earth. It is not that we do not have a mind and a heart. We know these things because we are alive and that Life is moving through our hearts, minds and bodies on Earth in this moment. Life is here. The Earth is here. Our mind is here, Our heart is here. **Where is the problem!?**

If we have a problem in our own experience on Earth, it is that our conscious mind is not really aware of the Source of invisible Life or really knows the Source of Life that is present. We do not know that we have this Power. We do not really know who We are!

The heart senses and feels that **Something** or **Someone** is missing but cannot define what it is. The purpose of the heart is to sense and to feel; the purpose of the conscious mind is to define and to understand and to explain. This should be our first clue that our mind and our heart are not in agreement. They do not know the **Operator** of the equipment that are using them! Since the heart and the mind are in the same physical body, they should be in agreement as they observe the one incident in the environment. It is possible that one of these capacities, either the mind or the heart, is not functioning properly.

 Here are several important questions for your consideration. Is it possible that mankind in general, and individuals in particular, could have been functioning **incorrectly** over many generations!? Could it be possible that in this **present** generation that individual minds and hearts of people are not functioning properly!? Is there a way to change the **improper** function of the mind and heart to a **proper** coordinated function of the mind and the heart.?

Is it possible that one of these capacities (the conscious mind) should be dominant and the other capacity (the heart) should be submissive to the dominant capacity as the **One** that we are observes the environment? If we are living in a lower world of turmoil and chaos that we have inherited and that we continue to make by our actions, (which is the land below the line), is it possible to fix the relationship of the disagreement between the mind and the heart as a requisite to begin ***LIVING IN THE LIGHT Above The Line!?***

More questions! Could the painful negative emotions that are experienced by the heart be **warning cries** that an Intelligent Source has built into the human form for the purpose of alerting the dominant conscious mind that it is the heart that is out of agreement with the creations of Life in the material world?!

Could this be the simple reason that human beings are indeed existing in this fallen condition which has been described as the Land **Below** the Line?! Would people be willing to repair the improper function of the heart if this correction was called to their attention!?

Would you!?

How does a polluted and an unruly heart become clean!? If the heart were cleansed and returned to its true position <u>above</u> the line, would it be in position to perceive the impulse of the invisible spirit of Life and also come into agreement with a conscious mind that is above the line!?

What has the mind been so busy doing that it has not asserted its dominant position in the physical body to discipline the unruly heart!?

Why hasn't the mind led the heart and the physical body to the place where human beings on earth can experience for themselves the art of *LIVING IN THE LIGHT Above The Line!?*

Who is going to show people the path that they can experience *LIVING IN THE LIGHT Above The Line!?*<u>How will you know if you are shown except by actually trying what you are shown in your own, heart, mind and body?</u>

Here are some <u>answers</u> for you to consider. The problem of the dominant conscious mind, which is separated from the flow of Life, that is Above the Line, is that the conscious mind has been busily engaged in judgment. The conscious mind has been and remains preoccupied with judging the forms--physical forms, mental forms and emotional forms--of the environmental world to be either "Good" or "Evil" forms. A mind that is busy **<u>judging</u>** the forms of the environment to be either "good" or "bad"--has no time to be creative and to <u>**serve**</u> the spirit of Life from above the line into the earth.

Actually, the earthly forms are never either good or evil: they are **perfect creations** of the forms which originated in the consciousness of the individuals who created them by using the power of Life. Why judge forms in the environment to be good or evil, why not simply observe these perfect forms for what they are and know that they are material designs that originated in consciousness?!. Your consciousness or the mass consciousness!

A conscious mind that is pre-occupied with the full time job of judging external forms of the environment to be either good or bad has little or no time to fulfill its primary purpose to be creative, to provide the designs in consciousness for the creations of Life that would be useful for people on earth. The mind has been **externally-oriented** to the already created things of the environment instead of **internally-oriented** to creating designs of beauty for the earth. This is a misuse of a mind that is primarily involved in external use that accomplishes nothing of value.

This habit keeps the mind off-the-mark, its primary purpose of creativity, so busily occupied with the forms of things that it does not have time to serve the purposes of Life to create fitting forms into the environment, which is the prime responsibility of Man and the human equipment. Man was created to be the **connecting link**, a human **being**, made of earthly forms and Life, to be Life's means of action on earth.

I repeat that it is necessary for the mind to come into agreement with the patterns in the environment because they are exactly what they should be according to the operation of the Law of Sowing and Reaping. It is logical and reasonable for the mind to come into agreement with the way things are in the environment because the environment in any given moment is **no other way** than the way it is. The environmental forms created from the designs in consciousness are to be perceived by the mind through the 5 senses of perception in the physical body. The information is then transmitted to the **One** within, You, for further creative purposes.

Initially, it takes some faith and discipline for the mind to come into agreement with the previously created material forms and transmit this information inwardly to the **One** within the form for further creative action. You must use the existing materials on earth to create new forms based upon a new design in consciousness. The mind understands that there is an orderly design behind the creation of everything. In the creative process, the mind deals with intelligence and logic; the heart, the emotional realm, deals with feelings and emotions of whatever is created in consciousness for the reproduction as material forms for the environment. The mind has a **dual purpose** on earth. The conscious mind has not been disciplining and directing the heart to the path that leads to the land above the line.

The **One** that we are is a spirit of Life in a human form even though we may not yet know this basic fact of our origin. As we assume an identification with the Spirit that is within the body, mind and heart, we are in position to direct the mind and the heart because Life is higher than form. The **One**, the Spirit of Life, **YOU**, can give orders to control, change and direct the feelings of your heart, the thoughts of your mind and the actions of your body **if you so choose**.

During many centuries of mankind living in the fallen state in the land below the line, we can honestly admit that the heart has become polluted.The emotional realm has changed from a heart filled with the positive emotions above the line at the time of our creation to a heart which contains the evidence of the **absence** of love and its many positive differentiations that we perceive as positive feelings. As the feeling of love is considered to be a **positive** emotion, the evidence of the absence of love can be seen as the **negative emotions** that we know as fear, greed, hate, jealousy, anger, resentment, disgust, worry, futility, frustration, apathy, etc. These emotions are not differentiations of love.

Our hearts are like the memory banks of a super-computer, which may have, somewhere in storage, all the events of the fallen state that may or may not be recalled. In addition to the facts of the distortions, the heart is filled with **emotions** that run rampant through the sub-conscious mind and they are free of association or attachment to any particular event.

Negative emotions are running randomly through the heart to reveal an impure heart. In addition to the negative emotions, the positive emotions of love, kindness, joy, praise, thanksgiving, serenity, friendship, etc. are also present to be experienced. The emotional heart contains both the positive and negative emotions to be called upon during the process of creation, or these emotions can be triggered to be released by our interactions and experiences with the people and things in the environment.

Consider a red, valentine heart as a material **symbol** of your own emotional heart. The heart has one small opening in its top which can be opened in two different and opposite directions: the heart can be opened **vertically** to the Source of Life in the physical form; or, the little opening can be directed **horizontally** toward the conditions of the environment of the material world.

In the fallen state of the land below the line, the **unstable** heart, with its one small opening, is open horizontally, and it can turn or rotate horizontally, 360 degrees in a full circle to view all the environmental objects to seek its earthly treasures. Generally, the heart is desirous of the "so-called treasures" of the material world of the environment to give it satisfaction or fulfillment. In severe cases, the heart can really lust after the material things of the world. The heart can be addicted to the things of the world and really hooked to drugs, sex, alcohol, gambling, chocolate, and a variety of activities which produce feelings of pleasure.

But the heart does not know that the feelings are not in the environment, the feelings are stored in heart and the subconscious mind and released from within. A person's heart can be open, horizontally, to the external treasures in the environment during every waking hour.

However, when a person is asleep, and the conscious mind has been put to bed, then Life has access to the little opening in the vertical heart and its emotions.

While the ideal position for a man or a woman is to let the vertical heart and the mind remain open to the flow of Life where the mind and heart can become nourished by the flow from the spirit of Life, it takes **practice and discipline** to maintain consistency. The Way is narrow. The tendency for an undisciplined heart is to return to the horizontal direction toward the environment where the **action** in material form is taking place.

In the fallen state, it is expected that people **"must react"** to the changing conditions in the environment. Everybody has been conditioned to react to their environments. "If you don't react to the things of the world, there must be something wrong with you. Are you dead or something." It is important to know that the **reaction** of a person to the environment will release positive and negative feelings and emotions from their storage place in the subconscious mind and heart. Addicted people get "GOOD and pleasurable" feelings from their habits before the evil negative feelings kick in as they are released. Our negative feelings are also stored within us.

All of us have had the experience of saying or doing something in the presence of another person who reacted in such a manner that they released one or more negative emotions of such intensity that we did not understand what had transpired. It is a common question to ask what **we** did to make that other person react in such a way that made them so angry, violent, mean, spiteful, jealous, hateful, bitter, etc. We cannot understand the human nature reaction of ill feeling because understanding is of the conscious mind and the feelings that are out-of-control are in a different capacity: they are in the heart, or the emotional realm.

Negative feelings can erupt from the heart like a volcano with the result that the person is in an upset state. The mind is supplying accurate information from one level of function, symbolized by the level above the Line, while the heart is functioning in a totally different lower level of operation, symbolized by a level below the line. The person in this condition is described as a house-divided: the heart in the basement and the mind on the upper floor. We can certainly see, that in the fallen state, there are many times when the mind and the heart are **not** in agreement. There are also times when the mind and the heart are **in agreement**. We have personal experience of both examples. We have never been taught how to be consistent.

A person whose mind and heart are going in two different directions--because the spirit of Truth in the mind is going in one direction and the spirit of a distortion of Love in the heart is going in another direction--cannot really be helped directly by someone else. It may be possible to restrain a person physically on occasion to protect that person or society, but the real controls located above the line within a person are accessible **only** to the **One** who inhabits the human equipment. No one else can really change your mind or your heart, except **YOU**. **YOU** are the **One**! The mind cannot change itself; the heart cannot change itself. **YOU** can change your heart and your mind which is the hope for your salvation from the fallen state. You have the ability to change your mind! You have the ability to change your feelings!

As **YOU** make changes in your heart and mind, **YOU** are expressing your Real Self of Life. The more YOU express your Real Self, the stronger YOU get and the more control YOU have over the human capacities of the mind and the heart. As **YOU**, the spirit of the **One** that YOU are, becomes stronger **through practice and experience**, then, the fallen human nature state that exists below the line becomes weaker. So it does benefit a person to practice the agreement of the heart with the mind.

The Disagreement between the heart and the mind is not the way to ***LIVING IN THE LIGHT Above The Line.*** Disagreement between the mind and the heart is always a painful experience. **The Way** to Agreement between the mind and the heart is not painful; it is pleasurable and it is easy. We need to learn the detailed instruction of how to keep our wayward heart in agreement with our conscious mind.

Chapter 7: The Agreement of Your Heart with Your Mind

Let us consider some simple exercises on how the **heart** can be brought into agreement with the **mind**. But first, let us use a new **symbol** to visualize the heart, the mind and the body. We have considered the symbol of the triangle with the base of the triangle representing the physical body and the two sides representing the mind and the heart to illustrate the three capacities which can be moved by the **One** spirit of a person, **YOU**, who were located within the space enclosed by the triangle..

Let us now use the figure **8** as a symbol for the physical body of a person, male or female, because each of us has a physical body. The figure **8** has the appearance of a "**Little Man**" to symbolize the physical body. The top circle of the figure **8** will represent the **conscious mind** and the bottom circle of the figure **8** will represent the **heart,** our emotional realm, with all of our feelings stored in the subconscious mind. The figure **8**, which appears as a "little man", will be our teaching symbol for the equipment of the spirit of Life on earth. The empty space inside the figure **8** and surrounding the figure **8 symbolizes the air of the Spirit.** The **8** is a teaching symbol of Spirit with a physical body with its mind and heart: **8 is a symbol of You above the line**. The three capacities of body, mind and heart are contained within the one symbol that is surrounded by the air of the spirit. Air is a symbol of invisible Life.

As our spirit with its heart, mind and body **8** observes the environment, we become aware of the patterns, the conditions in the environment, through our 5 senses of perception--sight, sound, taste, smell and touch--which bring information to our conscious mind, the top circle of the **8**. This information, particularly in relationship to sight and sound is vibrational: the information is in the form of vibrational light waves perceived through our eyes and vibrational sound waves perceived through our ears.

In this example, the light waves and the sound waves that we perceive are exactly what they are as they come to us from the objects in the environment; they have very specific vibratory rates, wave lengths, for each color and sound. It is important to understand that there is something very exact, very perfect, coming into the body from the environment and received by the 5 senses of perception and received by the mind and the heart We want them to be **in agreement with the vibrations from the environment.**

There is never anything "wrong" with the vibratory pattern whether it is an explosion or the sweet murmur of a baby. Vibrations cannot be "Good" or "Bad": they are the vibrations of the light waves and the sound waves which are perceived from the environment by **YOU**, **8**, the **One**. Our conscious mind receives this vibratory information and processes it into humanly comprehensible forms. This is one purpose of our conscious mind; to be aware of the conditions in our environment as they actually are. We work very well as the information comes into the minds of our physical bodies through our 5 senses of perception. We have received the vibratory information in the upper circle of the figure **8**, which symbolizes the conscious mind.

The information which is in the **mind** of the body is also to be considered, **secondarily,** by the emotional realm, **the heart,** symbolized by the lower circle of the **8**. The mind and the heart are connected at the intersection of the two circles of the figure, **8**. How do we "feel" about this information that the mind has received from the environment!?

37

If the information of vibrations of light from the environment is the color, blue as in a heavenly blue sky, and the conscious mind is aware that the color is blue, and the heart is **in agreement** that it is all right within the heart that the color is blue, (the heart likes the color blue), then, BOTH the mind and the heart are in **agreement** with the color from the environment. The result is that you are at peace with your environment. Everything's OK. God's in his heaven and all is right with the world as far as the color Blue and the heart are concerned

There is vibrational agreement in the environment, the mind and the heart. The result of this condition in the physical body is that the experience is one of mental **and** emotional acceptance, therefore your experience with the color blue is **acceptance, agreement and serenity**. The person is calm; the person is at peace with the environment. The heart is in agreement with the mind which is in agreement with the vibrations of color in the environment. This is an example of serenity. **Can you begin to get the idea that if you perceive that everything in the environment is exactly the way that it should be (according to the Law) then you will be serene and know serenity.**

Let us consider another person who is observing the exact environment with the exact same blue color of the sky. The conscious mind of the <u>second</u> person is aware that the color in the environment is blue which means that the conscious mind is aware of and in agreement with the fact that the vibration of blue is being emitted from the environment.

However, the **heart** of the second person doesn't want the color in the environment to be blue, the heart likes the color, Red as in a red sunset. The heart **wants** and **desires** to see **RED** as in a red sunset that produced a great feeling in the past for this person! In this instance, the heart is NOT in agreement with the mind. The emotional force of the heart is going in a different direction than the force of the mind with the net result that the two forces are going in opposite directions. This is an internal house-divided state.

This pulling of forces in <u>opposite</u> directions produce frustration and distress <u>within</u> the experience of the physical body; the feeling of distress is a **warning signal** that the heart is not in agreement with the mind. The person is a house-divided and the alarm has sounded. The emotions are "upset" and the alarms of negative emotions are sounded loudly. The calmness and serenity which is the true state of a Being in a human form has been replaced by irritation, anger, disgust, frustration and hatred which is directly proportional to the extent of how much the heart desires the condition in the environment to be something that it is not. The heart wants a RED sunset that is **not there** in the environment, and it doesn't want the BLUE sky that **is there** sending its vibrations of blue to the conscious mind. What a foolish heart. It needs disciplined.

Life disciplines the foolish heart, by releasing negative emotions from their storage area in the subconscious mind **whenever the heart is not in agreement with the mind**. Foolishly, the wayward heart is rejecting the information brought to it by the conscious mind. **The heart is objecting to its own state of consciousness when the heart rejects the information brought to it by the conscious mind.** Isn't this illogical!? The mind is logical., but the foolish heart wants its Good feeling from the Red sunset that is not in the environment. The heart is governed by feeling, not logic and reasoning.

The fallen self of the human **ego** that lives below the line does not understand how the equipment operates. The false-self does not understand that the negative feelings experienced in the heart are <u>warning signs</u> that the heart is not in agreement with the mind, and that some corrective action needs to take place to eliminate the warning signals of frustration and distress. The false-self of the fallen human ego does not know what to do.

The only thing that the false-self does know is that it **did not** have the experience of these negative feelings until the color blue put in an appearance in the environment. The false-self **blames** the color in the environment (which simply is the vibration of blue that it is) for creating the anger that is experienced by the false-self. "It was the color blue from the heavenly sky that caused these negative feelings in me". "That color made me angry!"

It is not uncommon for a person with the false-self, whose heart **wanted** the color Red so very much, to become red in the face, angry, and jump up and down in order to get what the heart desires. Immature children act this way. The false-self of the human ego throws a temper tantrum in a futile attempt to get the peace and tranquility which is the attribute of the True Self. Of course, the color blue in the environment cannot change what it is into a red sunset to please the desire of the heart, nor can the object in the environment ever eliminate the negative feelings that are stored in the emotional realm waiting to be vented. **It is impossible to please a desire of the heart that is not in agreement with the mind. The desire of the heart needs to change to agree with reality.**

The goal for true serenity is the **agreement** of the heart with a conscious mind that is in agreement with the reality of the condition in the environment which can never be wrong because the thing in the environment is what it is. The lack of agreement between the heart and the mind is always an "inside job" because heart and mind are within the body. The absence of inner agreement between heart and mind is always distressful. It is supposed to be! **It is a built-in warning mechanism!**

It is also possible for the heart to be in agreement with a mind that is **not** in agreement with the reality in the environment. For example, let us consider the situation in which the heart WANTS the color red so very much that it will not change to be in agreement with the mind and the false-self releases so many negative emotions that produce the torments of hell to the human body. The conscious mind then decides to move or change its correct and firmly held position of agreement with the object in the environment that cannot change.

Although the conscious mind was in agreement with the color Blue from the environment, the conscious mind, in order to end the distress, frustration and grief, decides to come into agreement with what the heart desires so very much.

The human ego control of the conscious mind will "agree" for the sake of "peace" in the body that it will come into agreement with the desire of the heart. The false human ego will command the conscious mind to deny the color Blue and call the Blue vibration Red in order to please the **desire** of the heart.. The human ego will do this. **The One never will!** The heart and the mind are now in agreement with the desires of the heart which removes the pressure of inner conflict on the physical body as the mental force and the emotional force are now in the same direction and not pulling against each other.

The mind and the heart are now in agreement with **an unreal state, a condition different that what is actually in the environment** and the person will be temporarily insane. The mind is not in agreement with the real condition in the world. This is an example of temporary insanity of a person who has "lost it", who has lost touch with reality but they are "happy" in their delusion of agreement in "left field", an unreal state.

These three examples, presented in the following illustration, are the ways in which the heart and the mind are: (1) in agreement with the **unreality**; (2) **not** in agreement with each other; or, (3) in agreement with the **reality**.

These three conditions of the mind and the heart within a human body can produce simple labels of (1) insanity, (2) stupidity or (3) serenity. The arrows used in the illustration are symbols of **forces** that have power: mental power and emotional power, which can either be in harmony with an unreal state, or in conflict with each other, or in harmony with a real state.

We need to learn to use our conscious minds correctly and to discipline our hearts to emotionally accept the information which the mind brings into the human form from any pattern in the environment made by the operation of the Law of Cause and Effect. A heart that desires an unreal condition in the environment needs to be disciplined immediately. The wayward heart must come into agreement with the conscious mind.

This agreement of the previously wayward heart with the conscious mind, that is clearly reflecting the environment, is the path to ***LIVING IN THE LIGHT Above The Line.***

Consider the following illustration of the 3 possible arrangements to understand how to live above the line. There is only one logical choice to make.

3 Possible Configurations of the Mind and Heart

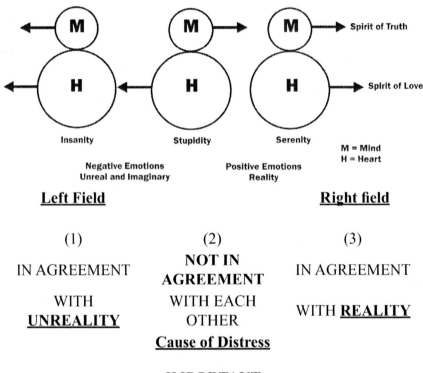

Left Field   Right field

(1)	(2)	(3)
IN AGREEMENT	**NOT IN AGREEMENT**	IN AGREEMENT
WITH **UNREALITY**	WITH EACH OTHER	WITH **REALITY**
	Cause of Distress	

IMPORTANT

Can you begin to see that when the heart is in opposition to the mind, when the arrows from the heart and the mind are moving in opposite directions, the body experiences Distress?Can you begin to see that your negative emotions are warning signs that your heart and mind are not in agreement with the real patterns in the world of your environment? (Figure 2)

Can you begin to see that when the heart is in agreement with the mind, when the arrows from the heart and the mind are moving in the same direction toward the real environment, the body experiences Serenity? (Figure 3)

Can you begin to see that when the arrows from the heart and the mind are moving in the same direction toward the <u>imaginary</u> environment, when the feelings of the heart with its foolish desires overpowers your conscious mind to achieve inner "peace", leads to a dangerous condition or temporary insanity in your body? (Figure 1)

Can you begin to see that the heart in agreement with the mind which is in agreement with the reality in the environment is the only "little man with both arrows pointed to the right" who is on the path to *LIVING IN THE LIGHT Above The Line*?(Figure 3) Can you begin to see that this "little man" is really the <u>One</u>!?

Chapter 8: The Philosophy of the Check Mark √

At the end of the previous chapter, we emphasized the necessity for the heart to emotionally accept the information which the conscious mind presented to it from the environment. It is true that to be ___LIVING IN THE LIGHT Above The Line___, the heart must accept the information that the mind presents to it through the 5 senses. It may seem to the reader that there is nothing further to be done after the heart emotionally comes into agreement with the mind which is accurately conveying the information from the structures and forms from the environment. Emotional acceptance is not the end of the story: it is only the beginning of a true creative process of really doing something productive and effective with regard to the forms of the environment. We can now begin to create **without using our negative emotions** which will pollute our actions.

As human beings, Beings in human forms on earth aligned with Life, we should begin to understand that our spiritual Selves are eternal while our human equipment is temporarily made of the atoms and the molecules of the earth. The spiritual Self or Being, present in every human form, is an aspect of True Cause. We symbolize the **One**, the Being that you are, as a "Little Man", an **8**, who is an individual aspect of Life.

Eternal Beings are either in form or they are not in form. Beings in forms are here on earth to bring a kingdom of order into the turmoil and chaos. The present chaos is the result of the original fall of man which we have described as the conditions which are observable in the land **BELOW** the line. How did the separation from the impulse of Life with the inevitable fall of man occur!?

When self-active minds and hearts contained in human bodies discovered that they had the "freedom" on earth to choose the treasures of the material world for self-satisfaction, to judge the things of the world as "good" and "evil", they began to eat of this Forbidden Fruit which moved their direct heartfelt connection with Spirit to the material world. They also chose to "forget" the reason for their mission on earth to bring the kingdom of the spirit of Life in the land above the line into physical form on earth . They chose to do their own thing, to ignore the Intelligent Designer Who sent us here, and to seek material treasures from the earth for their own gratification and personal self satisfaction.

Then, **chaos** resulted instead of divine order. The innate power to create was not lost but, instead of creating the beauty from heaven to the earth, the "fallen" horizontal hearts and minds, usurping the power of the Spirit of Life, created a terrible **distortion** of the kingdom of order, which is described by the words, chaos or hell. The consciousness of oneness with the Intelligent Designer, the Father of us all, was lost; the memory of the kingdom of heaven was lost; and the spirits in form on earth continued to create the terrible distortions which are now considered to be "normal behaviors".

Some religious people acknowledge the possibility of a beautiful kingdom of order, called heaven, but the idea of heaven is that it has become a special place that is not available for the people on planet earth while we are alive. Human beings in the fallen state have developed a belief system that the only way that Heaven can be accessed is through death, when their spirits, without human forms, will go to the heavenly place.The sincere belief of "going to heaven when you die" can prevent the possibility of experiencing the kingdom of heaven which is at hand, which is available to be experienced by **YOU** on earth while **YOU** still have a heart, mind and body to talk about it.

Other human beings have also developed another belief that there is no such place as a Land Above The Line, Heaven: it is a fairy-tale that doesn't exist and it can't be proven. Life on earth is the only experience. There is nothing else but the Big Sleep, Death.

These beliefs enable man, in his fallen state of consciousness, to continue to rule the earth as he has done in the past to create the distorted conditions that are observable everywhere. This decision keeps fallen man in charge, in some degree of control, here on earth where the hellish conditions of the land below the line exist and where they will continue to be made by present day behaviors. The people know earthly conditions are not heavenly but the fallen ego of man remains in control. The hellish conditions on earth are now seen as the product of "normal" human nature. It is a hellish and polluted state.

The place that we call Hell has been relocated by fallen man to a place that is accessible after we die, in the same manner that the entrance to Heaven has been relocated to a place that exists after death. Fallen man has accepted these "after death" locations because as long as he holds on to these beliefs, he is still in charge of the land under the line. Man in his fallen state developed an attitude that he would rather rule on earth in the hellish conditions which he calls normal, rather than to serve the spirit of Life from the Creator, which would actually bring the heavenly conditions to earth.

We advance the thesis that the application of the Law of Sowing and Reaping states that you know what you express and the personal application of this Law will be the Path to the proof of your actual experience. If you express the nature of the beauty of heaven into your environment, you shall surely know what you express and you will see the results of your beautiful expression while you are still alive.

If fallen man would serve and release the nature of the Father, a nature of Love, Truth and Life, then the consciousness of man in the fallen state would harmonize with the purpose of the Father, the Intelligent Author of the Divine Design. The result of this would be that the consciousness of man would be restored to the condition which it experienced and the position which it held **before** the Fall of Man occurred.

Of course, this restoration of fallen man cannot occur as long as the person wants to do his or her own thing instead of bringing the Spirit of Life from the Father into the earth once again. The idea of using the human equipment to serve the Spirit of the Father into the earth once again seems impossible to a person who has been trapped in the fallen state. It **is** impossible if man remains in the land below the line, who thinks that he is "only human, you know" and continues to act that way. There is no change.

In the previous chapter, we saw the need for a transition to occur in the consciousness of any person to move from identification with the earthly form of himself, the fallen human ego, to an identification with the spiritual nature that is also available to a person. Life is everywhere! The human self, trapped in the land below the line, imagines that this is really a very, very difficult thing to do.In actual practice, the Way is easy and the burden is light.

The person who begins to understand that His real Self is Spirit, and not the polluted human container, sees the transition as a simple step, from dwelling in the familiar troubled land below the line, produced by a troubled polluted consciousness of the person to the new and beautiful land above the line. The land above the line is created by the eternal Spirit that is the Truth, **8**, of each person.

A person's true nature is spirit which has the power and strength of Life if we choose to harmonize with Life. Fallen man is unfamiliar with the strength of Spirit because he is unaware of its presence, combined with the fact that nobody has shown him how to use it, the Spiritual Force. Scientists tell him that there is no such thing because you can't measure it, and the religious leaders do not demonstrate an example for him to follow.

The temporary self is a counterfeit experience which is really very weak. The counterfeit self must lose its life of falsity in order to experience the truth of Life. The step in consciousness from below the line to ***LIVING IN THE LIGHT Above The Line*** is only a choice away. It is very easy for man in the fallen state to return to the ascended state of the spirit because the ascended state is the **true condition** of man. Man is made in the image and likeness of the Intelligent Designer of everyone on the planet regardless of their beliefs or lack of beliefs. Man is here and he didn't create himself.

The Master Teacher, Jesus, said that the way was easy and the burden of spirit is light. Man in the ascended state knows his true purpose. The true purpose of man is to represent, **re-present**, the spirit of the Father on earth which is coming **directly** to you. **IF** we do this, we shall create a home, a place of beauty, using the spirit of the Father instead of the spirit of the fallen, self-active human mind polluted by negative emotions and influenced greatly by the so-called treasures of the material world.

The choice for each person is the creation of a world made by the spirit of God, **a spirit-made world**; or a world made by the mind of man in the fallen state, **a polluted mind-made world**. In either case, man will continue to be a **creator: a creator of destruction;** or, **a creator of beauty**.

If man chooses to be a creator of beauty, he cannot use the distorted good and evil fruit made through a polluted state of consciousness from the distorted environment as his starting point. He also cannot use the destructive emotions that brought about the present chaotic conditions due to the constant operation of the Law of Sowing and Reaping and hope to reap the kingdom of heaven on earth. We can see that **That's Impossible**

Fallen man has sown the wind of wrong expression, and he has reaped exactly what he has sown, the whirlwind, to create the conditions of the land below the line! Have you had enough of it! Risen man must sow His seed and He shall reap accordingly, which is the new state of ***LIVING IN THE LIGHT Above The Line***.

The only question is, What is the nature of the seed of behavior that is sown in consciousness? Is it the fallen state or is it the true state? True Man on earth carries the spirit Life from his Source, the Heavenly Father **(there is no other eternal Spirit)**, not the distortion of his earthly, heredity, the sinful, human-nature fathers of contemporary expression.

The true starting point for anyone and everyone, in any period of time, is that Man is made in the image and likeness of God, the Father. Man's spirit or Being is God's spirit or Being. Spiritual Man is the Rock, which is a small piece of the Mountain of God. Man is not the whole mountain of spirit, but he is a piece of the ONE MOUNTAIN. So is everyone in human form on earth. Each individual is a piece of the Rock. Each individual is the **One** Little Man, **8.** **Spiritual Beings in human forms**

The problem is that we have been hypocrites. We are spiritual beings who state that we are made in God's image, but we have acted as though we are "only human" and that we are filled with fallen human thoughts and the negative feelings that we must express come hell or high water. And, according to the operation of the Law; that's exactly what has come! We have been taught to worship our fallen human nature.

We deliberately did not choose to use our freedom of choice to express the nature of the spirit of the Father who sent us here to express ourselves as the children of God; but, we didn't know any better. Now, we can see more clearly and we **know** better. But, will we **DO** better!?

The only true starting point is to identify with the Source of your own Being. The true starting point is not to try to find the Garden of Eden, or the Kingdom of Heaven somewhere in the environment, by searching for it already completely built. The kingdom doesn't come by observation, searching here or there. The true starting point is the personal identification that **One** **is spirit** and that starting point **is** at hand, available. **We are not here to <u>find</u> the Kingdom of God; we are here to <u>bring</u> the Kingdom of God and live in the center of it. The True Garden is here and it can be experienced by *<u>LIVING IN THE LIGHT Above The Line.</u>***

As one identifies with the spirit of God, which is what YOU were created to be, and what you really are in Spirit, the person will express the nature of that with which he or she identifies. When people thought that they were only human, it was only natural for them to behave that way. It is the same process with the identification with the Spirit of the Child of the Father, the male or female offspring of God. A person who identifies with the spirit coming from God expresses the nature of God into the distorted world.

It is natural and easy for the spirit of God to express Love from God through the heart, Truth from God through the mind and Life from God through the physical body. The greatest obstacle is a concern with what other people will think of this strange behavior which has not been seen on earth since "the fathers fell asleep", since the fall of man. This book is a "wake-up call" for those who are asleep and who are willing to wake up and begin **<u>LIVING IN THE LIGHT Above The Line.</u>**

Man is a spiritual being with the divine ability to create. A spiritual being will <u>create</u> conditions that are true to the divine design of God using the attributes of God. A fallen human being will re-create and <u>copy</u> the things that are in the fallen mind, the fallen heart and the fallen world with great emphasis on **recorded history**. The recorded history is the history of the fallen state with flashes of light putting in an occasional appearance.

A <u>fallen</u> man opens his heart <u>horizontally</u> toward other people to try to make the people in the fallen state "happy", and to do what they would like for him to do to build the ideal world. An <u>ascended</u> man or woman opens the heart <u>vertically</u> toward the Heaven to let the spirit of Life from the Father flow into the earth which will bring heavenly conditions to earth. Do you think that you could choose to do this for just one fleeting moment!? How about **two** moments!? Getting the picture!?

This is not a new doctrine. Re-read the Lord's Prayer. The <u>spirit</u> from heaven comes from a vertical source but the <u>material</u> with which the spiritual being must work and function comes from the present material conditions on earth exactly the way they are in the environment in this moment and in every moment.

It is the spirit from heaven that descends vertically into the earth that will shape and lift the earth into new patterns and forms according to the operation of the Law of Sowing and Reaping to produce the New Heaven and the New Earth. As a person stands upright, to allow the flow of the spirit from heaven to flow into his body, the materials of the earth--physical materials, mental materials and emotional materials--are observed by your spirit of Life as building blocks for the new creation by the spirit through You .**8.**

Whatever material that is available in the environment is there as substance that is available for creation. The materials with which a person must work is what it is. Mother Earth. Matter isn't "Good" or "Bad", it just <u>IS</u>. The material forms are observed objectively as raw material for divine creation by You **8**.

The spirit uses the symbol of the Check Mark, ($\sqrt{\ }$), as a guide to creation. **The vertical line of the Check Mark symbolizes the raw material observed by you that is presented to the Child of the Father, the spirit which YOU are, as YOU begin to re-present the Father.You re-present the Father's spirit on earth, exactly where you are. <u>8</u>**

<u>The ascending line of the Check Mark,</u> that begins at the base of the vertical line and rises to the right and upward on an angle, is the symbol of the spiritual work that needs to be done by **YOU** on earth. The ascending line is the symbol of the function of your spirit on earth **to lift up** all the things of the earth as they pass through the heart, mind and body by your spirit Who is in form on earth as long as you are alive in a form.

The spirit, **YOU**, lift up the fallen pattern of the earth by the way in which the situation or circumstance is handled in your consciousness, using **your positive emotions** and **your creative mind** within **your physical body**. If you are praying for God to do it without your help, you are wasting your breath. He created you to do the **ground** work on earth.

In each and every moment that we are on earth in a physical form, we are at the **center** of the world of our responsibility. We always have an environment to "lift up" according to the symbol of the **Right Side Up Check Mark**. The symbol of the Check Mark should remind us that wherever we are, that we have the opportunity to lift up our environment in each moment because of our presence. As we are attuned to the flow of the spirit of the Father which is always coming down from God out of heaven as our daily (spiritual) bread, we will sense and know what to do in the moment. Check it out! √

There is no guide book for every action because no two environments are exactly the same for different people. Sometime the fitting thing would be silence; sometime a word might be spoken to uplift the situation; sometime the need for physical action can be taken. The answer will be made known in the moment as a person stands in re-presentation of the spirit of the Father for the purpose of lifting up the earthly circumstance because a Child of the Father is present. We are the children of God and our function is to lift up the conditions of the earth immediately around us, which is our only creative field of action.

In words that have been spoken before, the condition in the environment is to be observed, seen and beheld, exactly as it is. There is no need to judge the condition as "good" or "bad" because it is exactly the condition which is present in that moment that has been made by the operation of the Law in times past. If we judge the condition as "good" or "evil" for ourselves, then we lose our objectivity and we see the circumstance subjectively. Subjective vision is not objective vision.Subjective vision is not clear vision.

Your spirit can observe objectively to see clearly and exactly the circumstance that is present in the moment without judgment. It is the raw material from the fallen state that needs to be lifted up. It cannot be lifted up if we observe it subjectively and we have a personal desire to "put it down", or to complain about the way it is. The human self judges subjectively and is involved in putting down everything that is "bad" and lifting up everything that is perceived as "good" for "me", which is how the conditions of the world below the line became the fallen state. Everybody was putting everyone and everything up or down based upon our self-centered subjective judgments. Perhaps we can have a better understanding of what the Master Teacher, Jesus, meant when He said, **"<u>Behold, I make all things new!</u>"**

He made old things that were made by people in the fallen state **new** by the way in which He handled them and lifted them up as a representative of the Father on earth. He invited other people to do **<u>exactly the same thing</u>** because they, too, were children of the same Father. The Philosophy of the Check Mark is really another way of saying, **"<u>Behold, I make all things new!</u>"**

The Philosophy of the Check Mark is really very simple. Conditions in the present moment are the way they are based upon the operation of the Law. Conditions are not the way that you think that they <u>should</u> be **if only people had behaved differently; <u>people did not behave differently!</u>** They behaved the way that they behaved and that's what produced, and is producing, the conditions of turmoil and chaos of the land below the line!

Do not judge the conditions in your environment as "good" or "bad". The conditions are only atoms and molecules made by the action of the Law on the **mass** consciousness of mankind which includes **your** consciousness. You have a choice in each moment to let the spirit of God be <u>**a blessing**</u> in your real circumstances thereby lifting up the condition that is presenting itself to **YOU**. You can also view the very same condition, translate your perception of it **downward**, and be **a cursing** in your circumstance by condemning, complaining or "putting down" the conditions of the world that you center.

This latter action is the **Philosophy of the Upside-Down Check Mark** which is the choice that led to the fallen state. Man in the fallen state has his or her Upside-Down moments! There are many people in this world, and we have all been among them, who have looked at a situation as it exists in our environment and it has not been pleasing to us the way it is. We have not lifted that situation upward by our presence; we have put it down. In so doing, we have created a little more of the fallen state of mankind. We were creators of turmoil and chaos that produced this land below the line.

We have also seen a situation and lifted it up because of our presence. We have done both in our past experience. **These actions are not unknown to you**! We know when we have used the **Philosophy of the Check Mark** and we know when we have used the **Philosophy of the Upside-Down Check Mark**. If there is nothing that you can do about a situation, just be thankful that you can see it clearly and that the Law is in operation.

If **YOU** have the vision to see what needs to be done, **YOU** can choose to perform at the highest level of your vision. **YOU** have a choice as to whether or not you will **Live Above the Line.** You can also choose to remain in the land below the line. The Law of Sowing and Reaping shall continue to operate forever to remind you of your choice.

Chapter 9: Translating Our Perceptions of the Environment

In the application of the simple Philosophy of the Check Mark which was described in Chapter 8, we saw that the correct way to handle the circumstances that come to you moment by moment was to identify with your spiritual Self rather than the human self **before** you attempt to handle any situation or circumstance.

You are a **Being** in a **human** form. You are not "only human, you know". You will **never** get any experience of the Life of your Being by saying to your false self over and over again that, "I am only human, you know". When we do this, we are focusing our attention on the land below the line.

Next, we must observe accurately and objectively, the thing or circumstance in the environment exactly as it is. Physically, the object that is being observed is made of atoms and molecules that give shape and size to the object; the sights and sounds are perceived as vibrations of light waves or sound waves that are perceived by the two senses of perception used most often. We also have the sense of touch, taste and smell. Even the vibrations of another person's emotions can be perceived through your heart, your feeling realm.

Let us consider that we have made a videotape of the steps in the action of translating our perceptions from our personal environment.

Remember that the videotape is on **"Pause"** so that we can carefully study and examine the sequence of perception and the way that we observe our worlds from the <u>images</u> of the objects in our consciousness.

At the moment of observation, things are what they are in the material world **before** they are perceived by our five senses of perception. If we desire to function correctly, we must see things exactly as they are (objectively) and not the way that our heart desires them to be (subjectively) to please ourselves. Want and desire of environmental treasures create perceptual blindness in a person..

We have correlated the Philosophy of the Check Mark with the teaching of Jesus who said, **"Behold, I make all things new!"** as he lifted up everything in his environment in an ascending direction. This is the creative process of Blessing the particular world of our personal environment.

We are not so interested in **<u>receiving</u>** Blessings, but we are thankful if we do receive them from others. We are more interested **<u>in allowing</u>** the Blessing from the Spirit of Life pour into the Earth through the vessel of our heart, mind and body.

As a spiritual being on Earth who declared that he was in oneness with the Father, Jesus the Master Teacher would offer the Way of Life from the Father. Jesus exemplified the way for his disciples to "pray" the Father Who was within them.

Jesus didn't teach the limited instruction of **"My"** Father, which would limit the action of God to Him alone; he taught the doctrine of **"Our"** Father; which makes the power of God and the responsibility of man available to everyone.

As a spiritual being, we can symbolize the nature of our spirit as another triangle whose apex is pointed upward: the three points of the triangle represent the nature of the triune spirit, **the three spirits of Love, Truth and Life**, which are the **radiant** spirits that come from the Father to everyone.

The Father would not exclude His Radiance to any of His children. A person who represents the spirit of the Father must **re-present** the spirit of the Father through the human equipment, in any circumstance in which the person finds himself or herself.

It is good to know that we do not have to make or ask God to radiate his Spirit to us. God's Spirit is a Radiant spirit because His Spirit is always radiating to us in the same manner that the Sun is always shining on the just and the unjust.

We can use prayer effectively for ourselves if we pray to **turn our hearts to the Source** of the radiation that is within us. The radiation of the spirit from God has already been sent to us before we even ask. If we are asking Source to give us something special or anything at all, isn't that a sign that God has not provided for us? Do you have to pray for the Sun to keep shining!?

In any and every moment, we were created to receive the radiation of Light and apply the Power to translate the circumstances **UPWARD**. **The Operation of the Law** will guarantee that this action **will lift up** the condition by the very presence of a spiritual person, a person who is a receiver of the spirit through the heart and mind, by You, **8**.

The inner activity within a person who is observing the situation in the environment is symbolized by a **Check Mark** ($\sqrt{}$); the action in the present time is, **Behold, I make all things new**. The action 2000 years ago was, Behold, Jesus made all things new by the way he handled things. The action 3500 years ago was provided by the leadership of Moses in the way that he handled things. The actions 625 years ago was provided by the leadership of Mohammed in the way that he handled things in the spirit of Allah.

What was true representation back then to let the Spirit of the Father, Allah, come into the Earth is also true representation now. The Law of Sowing and Reaping did not change! The purpose of people to release the Spirit into the world did not change.

Of course, we are aware that many people do not choose to use their freedom of choice to "lift up" other people, circumstances and things in their particular environments. We have done it ourselves. In fact, we have done the exact opposite. We have **"put down"** people, places, circumstances and things; we have even been proud of our "put-down" skills. We have been proud to be "put down" artists.

Instead of the correct application of the Philosophy of the Check Mark which observed a situation objectively so that a spiritual person would lift up that situation to make it a better world because of our presence, we applied the **Philosophy of the Upside-down Check Mark** which "put down" the circumstance because of our presence. **This simple action created the land below the line, the fallen state of man. People have functioned as upside-Down Check Marks.**

We have observed the distorted circumstances of the world from a holier-than-thou position in which we thought that we were better than the people and the situations in which we found ourselves and, by our behaviors, we decided to complain and condemn the situation. Any person who behaves this way, which is a very common and prevalent behavior, is acting the way that "most people" behave in the fallen state because we are "only human".

When we behave this way, we do not re-present the spirit of the Father, a spirit of Love, Truth and Life; we represent an inverted triangle whose apex is pointed downward and whose triune spirits are characterized by the opposite conditions of **hate, lies and death**.

Whenever we hate being in a situation in which we find ourselves, we are expressing a spirit of hate from within ourselves; whenever we say that we should not be in that particular circumstance, we are lying because we are most definitely in the only situation in which we find ourselves in that particular moment, but we have not accepted the responsibility for being where we are and who we are. And, finally, instead of breathing some life into that particular situation, we have condemned it downward toward death, hoping that it would die so that we would not have to handle it correctly in the spirit of Love, Truth and Life.

These are always our **two** active choices in every circumstance: **a pro-active choice** is characterized by **Life** and uplifting the situation; or, **a reactive choice** is characterized by death and the defilement of the circumstance by putting it down even further than when we first saw it.. Life "lifts-up" the situation being observed into an ascending creative process; death "puts-down" the circumstance into a descending, destructive process that will ultimately destroy the circumstance in a disintegrative process. There is also a third choice.

The third choice, which is neither pro-active or reactive, is to remain on the fence and **do nothing** because of our own apathy. Do these three choices remind you of a practical scripture that teaches, **Either you are with me (Check Mark), or against me (Upside-down Check Mark); the lukewarm (do nothing), I vomit out of my mouth?**

The Check Marks have the effect of separating the sheep from the goats. The sheep follow the example of the Shepherd and do it the right way, while the goats "go-at" it, the environment, the wrong way. It is the goal that the sheep should become Shepherds!

At the very moment of observation of the situations and the circumstances in our immediate and personal environment which we center, we are in position to either lift-up or put-down the pattern in the environment. While we are in the "Pause" position observing our videotape so that we can analyze what is occurring, we can see an **upward triangle,** representing the spirits of Love, Truth and Life, that we have used on the occasions when we have lifted things up. Behold, I make all things new!The correct Philosophy of the Check Mark is in action through You when this occurs. You really do know this example when you have done it in your own experience.

We can also see that the **downward triangle**, representing the distortions of hate, lies and death, which we have used when we have put things down. We have seen the conditions in the environment as they are, and we did not want to begin our creation with the things that are actually in the environment; we want to begin with things that **we wish were there** as a starting point.

59

We want to begin to do our creative action with things that are not there; imaginary things; Behold, I want to begin with "new things" that are not there. Behold, I want to begin with new things, imaginary things, that would produce a much better creation than the things that are actually present. This is how we fool ourselves! We must always begin with the real circumstances that are present.

And so, the real things, which are actually present and which constitute the only real starting point, are not made new by our lack of creative action which would produce a new state, called the land above the line. The real starting point is rejected.

The starting point of the imaginary state is the way in which the person wishes or imagines that the conditions would be, so that we could do a much better job with a different starting point. **There is no different starting point other than the real condition which is present at the moment of observation**. Imaginary starting points waste your power which is used to produce unreal and distorted states on earth which are the real Hell on earth. The Land Below the Line becomes worse. The Law is always at work.

Whenever we use the starting points which do not exist to create the conditions of our particular worlds, we are **"Raising Cain"** (More about this later). Whenever we use our innate creativity using the spirits of Love, Truth and Life to make all things new, we are **"Raising Abel"** in the true creative process which could uplift the world and return conditions toward the Divine Design.

The fact that we see and hear so much about Cain, the allegorical symbol of the wrong behavior, and so little about Abel, the symbol of the right behavior, should give us some indication of what we are actually doing to maintain the land below the line on earth.

The Abel pattern is present as a seldom used potential. The Abel Pattern cries to us from beneath the ground where it is "buried" because the fields of Cain are so prevalent. We are either "raising Cain" or "raising Abel" with every action that we take in each and every moment. People are really proud of how much Cain they raised and they are pleased to give you all the details of their activities.

Which triangle do we use in each moment?Do we use the triangle of Love, Truth and Life with the apex pointed upward?Or do we use the triangle of hate, lies and death with the apex pointed downward?Which is the acceptable offering to Our Father?

In each and every moment of action, people with freedom of choice can choose to use either triangle. In our past experiences, we have used both triangles to translate our perceptions upward and downward.

We **know** both methods of behavior. We have **used** both methods of expressing ourselves. We create the polluted land below the line when we do.

When we have translated our perceptions **upward** using the spirit of Love, Truth and Life through the equipment of our heart, mind and body, we have been a **Blessing** to the world.

When we have translated our perceptions **downward** using the spirits of hate, lies and death through our hearts, minds and bodies motivated by imaginary and unreal starting points, we have been a **Cursing** to the world.

> **This is not a difficult philosophy to comprehend.**
> **In every moment, we are doing one or the other.**

No one is a cursing to the world consistently because we vacillate in our actions The question is, Is it possible to be a blessing to the world more consistently and more abundantly if we translate our perceptions through a triangle with the apex pointed upward?

The real blessing to the environment is to handle your affairs in the spirit of Love, Truth and Life through your own heart, mind and body. All it takes is some practice.

It is possible to merge the two basic triangles of the Radiant Spirit and earthly Form together, as shown in the illustration below. If we allow the triangle of Love Truth and Life with the apex pointed upward to descend downward about two-thirds of the way into the triangle of our physical equipment of the heart, mind and body (which was used for hate, lies and death) which is moving upward, we can choose to let the triangle of Love, Truth and Life merge into our own heart, mind and body. In this manner, the Radiance of Love, Truth and Life can manifest on earth in our own experience.

We can also see that the two **<u>separate</u>** triangles merge together to form a new six-pointed star. The Star is a heavenly body that shines its radiant light on earth. The two intertwined double triangles is the symbol which we know as the **Star of David** or **Solomon's Seal.** It is also the symbol of the covenant-agreement of the body of man from the Earth with the Radiance of Love, Truth and Life from the Father.

Take another look at the following illustration.

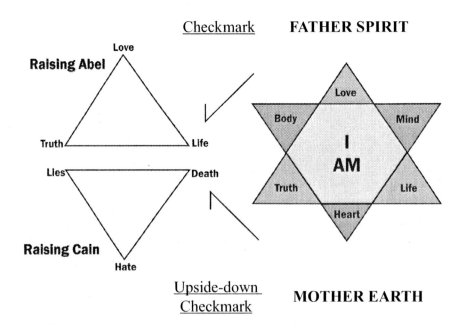

62

A person who wears the symbol of the Star of David suspended from a chain around the neck and attached to the apex of the upper triangle of Love, Truth and Life should be reminded to translate their perceptions **upward** in the spirit of the LORD, the spirit of the Father, so that they could be a Blessing to their world on a more consistent basis.

As this positive change occurs, the world of Cain (the world of the land below the line) would begin to disappear and the world of Abel *(the world of LIVING IN THE LIGHT Above The Line)* would begin to put in an appearance.

As we translate our perceptions upwardly on a more consistent basis, the Star of David can come to rest over our own heart in its true position. When this occurs, then we can understand that the Source of the Psalms, the songs of David, and the wisdom of Solomon came from the radiance of the Spirit through their human equipment. Can we begin to see that this same creative process that was available to David and Solomon is available to us today!?

The **center** of the Star of David is a symbol of a keystone where the spirit, where I Am, dwells. The center of the symbolic Star of David is the place where **I Am** dwells as far as **each individual** is concerned; the person who dwells there in the secret place of the most high is surrounded by the triangle of Love, Truth and Life that radiates forth through the heart, mind and physical body under control. A **Star of David** person is *LIVING IN THE LIGHT Above The Line.*

There comes a time in each person's experience when the creative triangle of Love, Truth and Life, which "raises Abel", replaces our expression of the destructive triangle of hate, lies and death that "raises Cain" because "raising Cain" is no longer acceptable to any individual who desires to remain on the spiritual path.

When you "raise Cain" you are off the Path! When you are off-the-mark, it is a **Sin**. When you raise Abel, the arrow of your expression is **In**., your expression is on-the-mark.

Cain and Abel were allegorical characters created by Moses, in his book of *Genesis,* who were born and lived together below the line or **outside** the Garden of Eden. The Cain expression became dominant in mankind and the fallen state of the land below the line resulted. As we learn to "raise Abel" in our momentary living, we **reverse** the process that led to the fall of man in our own experience. The Garden from which we fell begins to come into view and we, like the Prodigal Son, return to *LIVING IN THE LIGHT Above The Line*, which is the Garden, prepared for us by a Loving Father.

The "fallen state" condition, Raising Cain, was a **learned behavior** by man and this present, distorted way of the "fallen state" can be **unlearned,** if a person is willing. The true state of man was unlearned and forgotten in the past; the true state of man can be relearned in the present. True learning requires a transition from a state where the Truth of your Being is not known to a state where Something Special, the true state of man, becomes known. This transition can occur for you on Earth, this beautiful garden.

There was an experience **inside** the Garden before the fall occurred. Consistent expression of the spirits of Love, Truth and Life improves with practice. *LIVING IN THE LIGHT Above The Line* returns the individual to the state of living symbolized by the Garden of Eden.

Let's reconsider the following three illustrations from left to right that use two triangles to symbolize Raising Abel and Raising Cain; a Right-Side-Up Check Mark and an Upside-Down Check Mark to indicate our choices of translating our perceptions of the environment upward or downward so that we can choose this day which one we will use.

Consider the merging of the two triangles that portray the spirits of Love, Truth and Life flowing through the material form of heart, mind and physical body to form the **Star of David.** Put your Self, by saying I AM, in the keystone at the center of the Star. The Star of David is a symbol that represents the Covenant-agreement with God, the FATHER SPIRIT, the LORD Who radiates the Shekinah, the radiance from God, the Christ Radiance of His Love, Truth and Life into the MOTHER EARTH of each human person to create a Child of God in a male or a female human form.

A person who lives the Star of David would be a spiritual Son of David, a Son of the Covenant. That **One**, that person would be ***LIVING IN THE LIGHT Above The Line.***

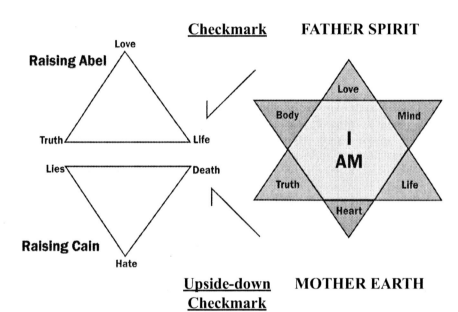

Can you apply these symbolic illustrations into the actual living experiences of your life on earth!? Raising Abel? Raising Cain?

The Philosophy of the Right-side Up Check Mark?

The Philosophy of the Upside-down Check Mark?

The Apathy of doing nothing?

The Spirit of your Father moving through your Mother Earth to create a Child of both Spirit and Form, You?

The Spirits of Love, Truth and Life moving through your own heart, mind and body?

Who is in the center of your individual Star of David?

Continue your journey by affirming, <u>I Am.</u>

This is the Way for you to be
<u>LIVING IN THE LIGHT</u> Above The Line.

Chapter 10: A Change of Heart

Let's review that every person has a physical body with a mind and a heart while we are living on earth. The heart, or the emotional realm, is a capacity through which we feel and it can be symbolized as a vessel, or a grail, which holds all of our positive and negative feelings and emotions. We could call this container of feelings an unholy grail that positions us in the land below the line!

While each of us has a heart, an emotional capacity, the emotional content of the heart is unique and varied to each of us. We might cast our minds back and imagine a time when man was first created, and in the **original state**, his heart was filled with love and all the positive differentiations of love, such as patience, kindness, understanding, compassion, forgiveness, joy, happiness, appreciation, tenderness, mercy, passion, etc.

These positive emotions would be the only contents contained in the vessel. There would be no negative emotions contained within the vessel of the heart. We can think of this container of original feelings as a *Holy Grail*! This is your true Spiritual Nature. This is what you really are. This is your True Identity in spirit.

At that time, each individual would be dedicated to the release of the spirit of the Father through one's own individual body, mind and heart. Since the nature of the Father is love, the release of the Spirit of God through the heart must be God's nature. God is love. If the person were also honest, and did not lie, cheat or steal, then these opposite distortions of the spirit of Truth would not be in the consciousness, or in the experience of a person either.

We can get a picture in our minds of what man, made in the image and likeness of God, might be: a heart full of the spirit of Love; a mind that is filled with the spirit of Truth; and a physical body filled with the spirit of Life. The conditions in the environment produced by the Spirit of Life would be characterized by what was in the consciousness of the original person or people.

A beautiful consciousness produced a beautiful world which was described by Moses as the Garden of Eden. This is a clear picture of the Land Above the Line and what is necessary for a person to enjoy *__LIVING IN THE LIGHT Above The Line.__* __Your heart longs for a return to this experience.__

Presently, after many, many generations of incorrect function, we are in a fallen state, and we are living in distorted environmental conditions symbolized by the land below the line. We have created these conditions through the operation of the Law which is never repealed as the Spirit of Life moves through the content of our consciousness. We are certainly not living in the state of <u>the land above the line</u>, We have fallen quite a long way from the ideal state that was called the Garden of Eden in the Book of *Genesis.*

Today, we can observe a very distorted state, a fallen state, that we do not have to imagine. We just need to look at the world of our creation through our consciousness, or, at ourselves if we are honest enough to look. The whole world is in the fallen state. See it for what it is. Don't feel bad about it! Certainly, we could have made it much better if we knew better. But we didn't know better. Let's be thankful that we can see it clearly now.

What is it that has changed over the centuries since man was in the Edenic State!? Certainly, we can see that it is the mass consciousness in general, and the hearts and minds of the individual person, in particular that has fallen from LIVING IN THE LIGHT Above The Line to the land below the line which we are leaving.Prime emphasis can be placed on the addition of the negative emotions in the land that we are leaving to the positive emotions of the True State that were originally in the heart.

The heart of a person today is filled with the positive emotions that were in the original design, but now, over many generations, we have added the other negative emotions such as fear, greed, anger, resentment, jealousy, hate, disgust, bitterness, harmfulness, spite, irritability, etc. Regrettably, we now consider this condition to be "normal". (I trust that you are beginning to see it as **polluted**.)

The result is that our hearts are filled with a mishmash of emotions of all sorts. Some of us are even proud of the negative characteristics which have been passed down to us for generations. We have these particular characteristics because we are certain nationalities, or colors, or creeds, etc. "These are the reason why we have these strong negative emotions and we lose our **cool** so easily. We inherited them from our forefathers. We've always been this way." These statements reveal that we intend to remain the way we are.

"Cool" seems to be an acceptable buzzword for the **positive** emotions; and "Hot" seems to be an apt description for the **negative feelings** that "burn" us while they are in our bodies and as we express them to others. The amount of **discomfort** or **comfort** associated with the emotions may have a great deal to do with the symbolism of the burning fires of hell and the coolness of the moist, white clouds of heaven. The presence of the various positive and negative emotions within us are directly related with our comfort and discomfort.

Let's take a look at the emotions in our hearts. If we were to list all of our present day emotions, both positive and negative, known in the experience of men and women and place them on a blank page, we might learn something of the emotions in our own hearts.

In the fallen state where we live below the line, we are quick to take credit for our positive emotions, but the negative emotions that we experience are almost always the fault of someone else. This should give us a clue that we deal with our positive and negative emotions differently.

There is a tendency for us to blame others for causing our negative emotions, or, to say that we are this way because we inherited these traits from our forefathers. We've always been this way, normal for us, for as long and as far back as we can remember.

See the following illustration for a partial listing of our positive and negative emotions. Emotions are powerful so I will list both positive and negative emotions in **Boldface type**. You can add a list of your own to these.

<u>Emotions in the land below the line.</u>

LIST OF EMOTIONS STORED IN YOUR HEART & KNOWN IN YOUR MIND

Love Hate Kindness Guilt Peace Revenge Appreciation Anxiety Joy Blame Delight Resentment Forgiveness Grief Comfort Sadness Approval Fear Truthful Resistance Worth Discomfort Happiness Apathy Serenity Despair Industrious Irritability Ecstatic Disgust Patient Insecure Thankful Hopeless Lighthearted Greedy Glorious Worthless Satisfied Disappointed Fulfilled Laziness Trust Helpless Supportive Victimized Resilient Stubborn Confidant Frustrated Capable Empty Willing Worried Blessed Cursed Order Chaos Thrilled Confusion Repentant Sinful Creative

Notice the mixture of positive as they are presented and negative emotions as they are placed very close to each other.

Let's create another list.

If we were to list all of the <u>positive</u> emotions known in the experience of men and women which are pleasant and place them

70

on the upper portion of a page **above** a horizontal line, and we list all of the <u>negative</u> emotions which are uncomfortable and place them on the lower portion of a page below a horizontal line, we might learn something from the new arrangement of the emotions in our consciousness.

Let's look at the new arrangement.

Consider this rearranged listing of the very same positive and the negative emotions.

<u>LIST OF EMOTIONS STORED IN YOUR HEART & KNOWN IN YOUR MIND</u>
Positive Emotions: <u>Heavenly</u> Blessings

love	kindness	peace	appreciation	joy
fulfilled	glorious	delight	forgiveness	comfort
gladness	approval	truthful	light-hearted	worth
happiness	serenity	trust	satisfaction	resilient
confidant	ecstatic	patient	supportive	thankful
capable	willing	orderly	industrious	blessed
thrilled	repentent	creative	courage	

Negative Emotions / Painful Blessings

hate	guilt	revenge	resentment	blame
anxiety	grief	hopeless	dissapointed	worthless
greed	fear	apathy	resistence	despair
furious	disgust	insecure	discomfort	laziness
helpless	victimized	stubborn	frustrated	empty
worried	cursed	chaos	confusion	sinful

Please note that the Positive Emotions <u>above</u> the horizontal line remain in Boldface Type

Also note that the negative emotions below the horizontal line are in italics

We know what it is to accuse and blame others for "making" our negative feelings when they arise from our own subconscious minds and hearts to the level of our conscious mind. We really do sense or know that all our feelings are our own and that we do not get our personal feelings from someone else. We need to acknowledge their presence in our hearts and accept responsibility for them. We can admit that all of these emotions exist and they are known by us in the land below the line where we and others dwell. These emotions are in our hearts and we accept responsibility for them. Our emotions are **our** emotions.

If there once was a state on earth, in which the heart was filled with **love and the positive emotions,** would it be possible to begin to return to that state once again? Would it be possible to begin to change the mixture of the positive and negative contents of a person's heart deliberately in an orderly and scientific manner? Why not!?

There would be no need to let go or release anything positive, right or desirable; but, we might want to eliminate the emotions that were unpleasant, harsh, mean and nasty **if we knew how to do it. There is a Way to do this. We can begin by letting the Spirit of Life that is coming to you flow through you.**

Slowly, we would experience and know our own negative emotions as they surface from their storage place in our sub-conscious minds whenever the heart was **not in agreement** with the mind, a mind that is in agreement with the actual condition in the environment. The negative emotions would be released as an uncomfortable emotion in protest from a human nature standpoint, or as a warning signal from a higher level of consciousness.

For example, our car has a flat tire, and our conscious mind is aware that the tire is flat. **But** the heart **wishes** that the tire were not flat thereby placing the heart in **disagreement** with the mind. In this condition, we are upset and we know the unpleasantness of the disagreement between the mind and the heart.

When the heart wishes that the tire were not flat, a negative emotion of anger or irritation arises from our subconscious mind and **seemingly** attach themselves to the external event in our consciousness as the "reason" for our being so upset.. **The flat tire made me mad. There are no feelings in the tire. The feeling was in us and it was triggered or released by the event. The flat tire was an external trigger to release an internal negative emotion from the subconscious storage place. This is the way it works.**

The real reason is that the **heart** is rejecting, rather than accepting, the information that has been presented to it by the conscious mind. The tire is really flat. When the heart rejects the true information from the conscious mind, a negative feeling is released from your subconscious storage place in your heart. When the negative emotion is released from your subconscious mind, you are now aware of the feeling in your conscious mind..

This conflict is an "inside job". The heart is not in agreement with the mind and a negative emotion has been released to warn you of this condition of internal conflict. **What can we do with this negative emotion of which we are now aware?**

There are 3 ways of handling the negative emotion: the first two ways are incorrect and they will keep you below the line; and the third way is correct and using it will move you above the line. (In all three examples, the tire is flat and it has to be repaired!)

Example 1. We have a flat tire and we experience a negative emotion. We are the only person in the car who has a negative emotion to deal with. We can rationalize our present situation and function as we always have in the past with the expression, "Well this is the way I am when I get a flat tire, I automatically get this negative emotion! I've always been this way. My father was this way too" This behavior acknowledges that the negative feeling is at the level of the conscious mind, but when we say that this is the way we have always been, we are **re-inserting the negative feeling back into the heart** where it will resurface again later.

When you use this example, you have created a **loop effect** for a feeling that came from the subconscious mind, then it rose to the level of the conscious mind and then, you reinsert the negative emotion back into your heart. **There has been no change of heart.** (The title of this Chapter is: A Change of Heart.) This method is unsuccessful.

Example 2. We are consciously aware of a negative emotion **that we feel after our conscious mind reveals to us that we have a flat tire.** (We may not be aware that all of our emotions are internal to us.) We rationalize that we didn't have this negative emotion **until** we had a flat tire. We incorrectly rationalize again, that since we didn't have the feeling until the very moment that the flat tire happened, then the event of the flat tire **made** the negative emotion which is uncomfortable and painful to us.

Whenever we do this, we have just **blamed** an <u>external</u> event for making a feeling that is <u>internal</u> only to you. Blaming and accusing your external circumstances as the **<u>cause</u>** for your feeling is not true. The negative feeling did not come from the flat tire or your environment. The feeling was released from within your subconscious mind where it has been stored for years. This method does not clear the heart and the person will continue to act the same way in the future.. There has been no change of heart. (The title of this Chapter is: A Change of Heart.) This method is unsuccessful

Example 3. A person does have the ability to accept responsibility for the feelings of anger and irritability that come out of the person's subconscious mind, and then release these negative feelings with a feeling of thankfulness: such as, **"I am thankful with my heart that I can see clearly that my tire is indeed flat. The event of the flat tire released negative emotions from my heart."** If this is done just one time, we replaced anger with calmness and the condition of the heart has changed. We can affirm that I do not want hold on to that anger that came from my heart to the level of the conscious mind and I will release it and throw it away.

Personally, when I experience a negative emotion, I declare, **"Get out of my house, you louse "** It is a lousy feeling. You don't reinsert it down into the subconscious mind again. You also don't hold it in which is putting the "lid on the id" to create a pressure cooker effect. You don't blame anyone else or any thing for making this lousy feeling. Just recognize it, release it, and let it go because it is not your True Nature.

The result of this deliberate action by the conscious mind is that the heart is lighter, less inflamed, less apt to explode into an emotional outburst. Calmness puts in an appearance. Of course, you don't have to change your heart if you don't want to. But who is suffering over and over again if you don't do it!?

The key to the change of heart is to be alert to the nature of one's own expression. If a person is aware of a negative emotion in one's own experience, it is very wise to accept full responsibility for that emotion as erupting from one's own subconscious mind. The negative emotion that you feel is not "made" by someone or something else in your environment: the ill-feeling was recalled from the reservoir of one's own heart and attached to the image of the external event by you, a false sense of self.

If you do this, if you accept the unpleasant, negative emotion as one's own feeling, realize its source, and **discard it**, let it go, and it will pass away from the heart. This is the first step in sending one's heart to the laundry, or allowing one's own heart to be cleansed. The goal is purity of heart. As you read these words, you can begin to release all the negative emotions that have been polluting mankind for generations. Your little thimbleful of consciousness is being cleaned. The mass consciousness is also being cleaned.

This is a major step in the creative process of ***LIVING IN THE LIGHT Above The Line*** for yourself and all mankind! We are moving toward an experience in living on earth with the way things are without the negative emotions to weigh us down.As you release your hold on the negative emotions, you shall feel lighter when you choose to express a positive emotion.

It is impossible for you or your conscious mind to get hold of any of the negative emotions that are stored in the subconscious mind. They are **sub-conscious**, below the level of the conscious mind, where they are not accessible to the conscious mind. We can't get into our subconscious mind to clean it. We must deal with the negative emotions **whenever they surface** from their lair. Negative emotions are as dragons that belch the hot fire and smoke through our own bodies **before** they can be expressed externally to others.

The negative emotions will surface at the most unexpected times. The "bigger" the event in our self-centered world, the larger the "dragon" of the negative emotion that erupts from us with its fiery breath to burn ourselves and others. But we can't burn others without the negative emotion burning ourselves, our minds and bodies, on the way out of us. The conscious mind knows this. The conscious mind knows what feeling that was expressed from the sub-conscious mind on its way into the external environment.

Consider these other examples that are greater than a flat tire. A jumbo jet airplane crashes into a skyscraper!The assassination of a president releases powerful negative emotions from your subconscious mind!If a person is totally unaware of the event that has taken place, there is no discomfort in the mind and the heart of the person **who does not have this information**.

But once the conscious mind receives and transmits the information to your heart that a president was assassinated or the jumbo jet has crashed, then the mind and heart, your consciousness, is aware of the unchangeable event that occurred in the environment.

However, the heart does not want to believe this "terrible" news presented to it by the conscious mind. The heart does not want to accept **emotionally**, the fact that what it heard through the conscious mind was the unchangeable fact of the matter, the actual condition in the environment when the event transpired. The event occurred in the environment based upon the Law.

Murderers commit murderous acts. The **images** of what happened in the environment has been transmitted to your consciousness. The images of a plane hitting a building is engraved in your mind and heart. They are graven images. They are to be seen and not worshiped,

The predictable sequence of events when the images are received by the heart are threefold: **disbelief, shock and a negative emotion**. The heart of the false-self of a person who dwells in the land below the line does not want to believe that a president had been assassinated or a plane was deliberately crashed into a building killing innocent people. The heart does not want to believe the information brought to it by the conscious mind. **(Disbelief is the first sign of a wake-up call to bring the heart into agreement with the conscious mind)**.

The second step in the process is that the physical body experiences distress and shock because the heart is **resisting** the information which has been supplied to it by the mind of an event that has already occurred in the environment. **(Shock is the second wake-up call to bring the heart into agreement with the conscious mind)**.

Finally, a negative emotion of anger, hate, or irritability that is released from the sub-conscious mind is further evidence that the heart is not in agreement with the mind. **(The negative emotion is the third wake up call to bring the heart into agreement with the conscious mind)**. The heart is supposed to accept the correct information brought to it by the conscious mind otherwise the heart is objecting to its own state of consciousness.

If these wake-up calls are really necessary, then the person should begin to be aware that they are asleep on the job of caring for the correct operation of the heart and the mind. People who dwell below the horizontal line should come to realize that they are indeed asleep at the switch. The switch is the interface of the heart with the mind, the lower circle of the **8 symbolizes the heart; the upper circle of the 8 symbolizes the mind**. The mind and heart should work together for proper function.

The negative emotion can be anger that we live in a world where such terrible things can happen; or hatred against the person who committed the crime; or blame and accusation that the people assigned to protect us did not do their jobs. None of these feelings can ever possibly reverse the event that has occurred. Bullets that kill people or planes that are driven into buildings NEVER back up.

It may seem to take "**time**" for the heart to come into agreement with the mind to accept the fact that the terrible events occurred. **Actually, emotional acceptance is not a function of time; it is a function of emotional acceptance by the heart.**

Consider this true story of a woman who lost her son (my godfather) in World War II only seven days before the war ended when he was killed by a sniper. She wore black clothes and lived in terrible sadness for over 40 years! Is 40 years too long to mourn?! How about 4 years?! 1 year? Twenty weeks? One month? Two weeks? Of course, she and her conscious mind knew that her son was dead, but her heart never emotionally accepted the fact and she remained heartbroken until her death

Can you begin to see that the healing process is **not a function of time** but a matter of the heart accepting what the mind knows to be true because the actual circumstance that occurred will be no other way? It is possible to **emotionally accept** with the heart the information from the **conscious mind** of the death of a person in the **environment** more quickly because the death event is irreversible and it must be accepted by the heart sooner or later. When the heart accepts the information, the pain goes away and the comforter, the Spirit of Truth, puts in an appearance.

The sooner it is done, the sooner **YOU** get over the sadness of your negative emotions and return to the acceptance of a positive emotion from the land above the line. **Acceptance** of the ways things are is a positive emotion. Never forget that the Being who you thought died, **never** dies; the spirit of the person is no longer in a physical form.

Actually, a time of trouble and shock releases many negative emotions from the reservoir in which they are stored: **the polluted heart of the subconscious mind**. This flood of grief and negative emotions can be used creatively as a means of recognizing the negative emotions that are stored in the subconscious mind. It is an excellent opportunity to clean them out and discard them from the house of one's Being.

Discard them from the house of your Being! Is this done to produce a cold-hearted, impassionate, unfeeling person?Or, is this done to give Life a clear channel to use on earth to help other people by delivering the truth of Life to those who are hurting and in need?

We need to keep in mind that the children of God are spirits that can not be harmed by the death of the physical body. If the truth of a person survives at death, then a person who is sad and unhappy is crying for himself, his personal sense of loss and his own fear of death. IF Beings on earth in form survive the event of death, then, Death, where is thy **sting!?**

The kingdom of God is a kingdom of Life. Life cannot die. "Dead" life is a contradiction in terms. The nature of Life is to live and to be alive. The spiritual child of God is eternal. Do not judge by the appearance of the physical form. Judge righteous judgment. The children of Life, the children of God, are either in form or not in form. The Children of God, like God, continue to live.

Instruction has been given to have a change of heart. Why?!Blessed are the pure in heart for they shall see God. Is that enough reason to let your heart be cleansed of the pollution of the centuries?Is that enough reason for you to **Let not your heart be troubled**?**YOU** are the only person who has access to your heart.

As the heart of a person releases it hold on its troubles, its negative emotions, by letting go of them, then, it becomes **untroubled**: an untroubled heart. It is possible for an untroubled heart to exist amid all the mess of the environment, **in** the world of distortion and chaos, but not **of** it. We live in a modern day world of distortion, turmoil and chaos. We were born into and we have functioned regularly in the land below the line.

A person with a real change of heart would be a new person and he would be a citizen of the new Kingdom who is ***LIVING IN THE LIGHT Above The Line***. The new kingdom is only **symbolized** as the land above the line. There is a Real Kingdom to be experienced on earth and it is at hand, which means available. Instead of being a member of the body of fallen human beings, he would be a member of a new body on earth which is not the body of the people who live below the line in the fallen state. It is the body of people that Intelligent Life has designed to live on Earth. A person does not clean out his heart for himself; he does it so the Intelligent Designer to have a clear channel, to shine on Earth, a straighter pen, to write with on Earth.

An invitation has been set before **YOU**, your physical body, your mind and your heart to take the step toward ***LIVING IN THE LIGHT Above The Line***. The invitation implies that you must leave your painful, negative emotions behind you. The negative emotions are available as a warning sign to alert you that you are functioning **below** the line.

Negative emotions are a warning for you to step over the horizontal line immediately to where you really belong.

Chapter 11: Negative Emotions: Painful Blessings

Finally, at long last, you have a logical answer to some questions that may have been bothering you all of your life! Questions, such as, "If God is so all good and perfect, then why did He create me in a manner that I could feel so miserable, fearful, worried, angry, hateful, resentful and all these uncomfortable negative feelings?" "Why did God or Life make me this way?"

Now, you have a logical answer. **He did it to protect you!** He did it to protect the Spiritual You, the Spiritual Self, from your false "only human" self! The false self that would surely result if mankind would choose to turn away from God and **choose** to desire the so-called treasures of the material world. This turning away from the Source of Life would automatically remove Man from his high position in the covenant-agreement with God in His Heaven of the Land Above the Line to a lower position in the material earth.

Man in human form, symbolized by the allegorical story of Adam and Eve, moved out of the Father's House to the land below the line as they turned their hearts and their backs to God. If your present experience is one of living in the land below the line, you can be certain that you have lost your connection with Life, with the Source, God, the

Intelligent Designer. You have been attracted and mesmerized by the material world which is only stuff made of molecules.

A Perfect God would do this to protect You. A God of Love, Truth and Life would build a protective device, a warning system, a sensing mechanism to alert His creation made in His image. God, the Creator, the Intelligent Designer, knows how to do this. God is Pure Love in all its positive differentiations. God is the Light and the Bright Force. God has no negative emotions.God is Love. The power of Love is the Force of Life.

Yes, there is a dark side of the force which produces the negative emotions and conditions in the land below the line by the operation of the Law of Sowing and Reaping. The experience of the dark side of the force is not **God's** wrath; the wrath is at the material level outside the spiritual Garden. The wrath is the warning sign that man, male and female, has chosen to move away from where he **should be** in relationship with the Living God that is symbolized by the words, ***LIVING IN THE LIGHT Above The Line.***

The out-of-position experience of the conditions of turmoil, chaos and distortions are called, "Raising Cain". The distortions are the evidence of the absence of the Truth of Love which has always been available to be experienced as people return to the LIGHT that is in the Land Above the Line which has always been available, at hand, to be entered into.

There is a need for the Prodigal Son to leave the land below the line and to return Home to the Land Above the Line and be welcomed by His Father Who has never moved (He never will!) from above the line. The Father will not punish His wayward son. The son has been punished enough by his own actions in the land below the line! Home, or Above the Line, is on this side of the grave as well as on the other side of the grave. Spiritual Home is everywhere. God is everywhere!

You have already seen that the human mind had to be free, free to create, free to choose information from the memory banks where the information is stored, free to reason, free to make Man the crowning creation of life on earth as a Co-Creator with God.

In this freedom, man is free to create the things of God on earth which are things of beauty and perfection. Man is free to create the divine design on earth in material form using the spiritual design, which is present in the heaven, the land above the line, that has been created by God.

However, along with the freedom to create things of beauty when Man is <u>with</u> God, in vibrational attunement and harmony with God's Radiance, the mind of man is also "free" to create things which are **not of God**, things which are not of the divine design. The mind of man in the fallen state is "free" to be attracted to the material things of the world. The mind of man is "free" to live off-the-mark, in Sin, to murder, hate, lie, commit all kinds of destructive acts to get what it wants, **the divine experience**, from the material world. Of course, the divine experience is not available in the land below the line, the fallen earthly conditions.

A God of Love would never do these things. God is a God of Love, Truth and Life: not a god of hate, lies and death. God built and owns the material world of atoms and molecules and He is wise enough not to descend into it and worship His own creations. God knows enough to use the material world to create forms of beauty.

So God put **a mark** on the allegorical fallen child of Adam and Eve, **Cain** so that none, no one, should harm him.Cain, the allegorical symbol of **wrong expression,** is the murderer of his brother Abel, who is the allegorical symbol of **right expression**. The offering of Abel, not Cain, is acceptable to the LORD.

Cain is a warning sign of the wrong expression, the wrong creation, to warn us whenever we were creating something which would have a harmful effect upon the body of mankind which includes us in this present day. **The Mark of Cain is the presence of the negative emotions in the heart which is then built into all material creations.**

This mark is recognizable world wide. The Mark of Cain is a universal mark that is applicable to everyone on the planet. It has been so universal for such a long period of time that almost everyone considers the destructive behaviors produced by the negative emotions to be "normal".

We're all "normal", which means, mediocre. "We're only human. you know." This is the fallen state of man speaking, raising Cain, and he dwells in the land below the line exactly where we are today. We are the offspring, the descendents, of the Cain state who should choose to return to the place from which we fell. This is fallen "Human Nature", the nature that has been built without the Intelligent Designer.

Science teaches us that all ideas should be put to the test to verify or disprove the validity of the data. We have a **symbolic interpretation** of the Mark of Cain which is a revolutionary idea that must be tested against the **literal** interpretation of Cain. The literal interpretation of Cain has problems: Where did Cain's wife come from!?

Even though you may "feel" that the symbolic version of the Mark of Cain is true, it must be tested in the laboratory of life. Each of us is our own laboratory. Each of us has a body, mind and heart and each of us has experienced the negative feelings, the negative Cain indicators which compose the Mark of Cain.

The beauty, the simplicity, the orderliness, the sense of the fitness of this concept deserves a trial by all who are willing. Special efforts should be made, not only by people in the scientific community but also by the people in the religious community. particularly Jews and Christians.

The story of Cain is a religious story from the Book of Genesis and we know that there is a tremendous love for God by religious people. Since the story of Cain appears in the Old Testament of the Holy Bible, which is acceptable to Jews and Christians, there should be a few people who might be willing to participate in a test to determine whether or not the negative emotions can be used as warning sign to indicate individual wrong behaviors in one's individual expression.

It would only take a few Jews and Christians to temporarily set aside their strong traditions and firmly held beliefs long enough to test the theory of an Intelligent Design (Man) and an Intelligent Designer (God) which should lead to Oneness and Unity of Man with His Creator, the Covenant experienced by Abraham on this side of the grave.

In order to participate in such a test, both the scientists and the religionists must admit that they have negative emotions and that they are willing for them to pass away from their present experience of life. Their hearts would be cleansed in the process.

This interpretation, that the Mark of Cain is a composite of all the negative emotions which produce distorted behaviors in human beings, is not presently the majority opinion of religious scholars. Science teaches us that the majority opinion is not necessarily right. What is the truth?! Beliefs may not be the Truth. Religionists have said that God made man and God doesn't make junk. Religionists teach that Man is not the haphazard product of the theory of evolution: he has an immortal spirit which is part of the Spirit of God. Is anyone willing to prove it in one's own equipment?

Science believes that there is such a thing as "normal" anger because the evidence is in their favor that everybody has it, and they have studies to prove that anger exists in everybody. Mankind has been "Raising Cain" for a long time, for as far back as we can remember.

Is it possible for a person to use his or her freedom of choice to deliberately choose NOT to express the negative emotions by not reacting to the patterns of material world made of atoms and molecules?Are the negative emotions a learned behavior that can be unlearned and eliminated from a person's expression of life with sufficient practice?Can the elimination of the negative emotions be used to protect God's creation, Man, male and female?Can we learn to say good-bye to the Raising of Cain within ourselves?

What would happen to a person who consciously decided with all of his mind and all of his heart to stop "raising Cain"? Would he explode from keeping the "lid on the id", keeping the cover on the negative emotions stored in your subconscious mind? This has been a premise of science. They say that it can't be done, whoever "they" are. Or, if it could be done, would a "new" person appear in our own experience? Or, would it be not a new experience, but the original creation? Or, if man fell from the Garden State while he lived on earth in the past, then, why can't he ascend to the hill or the high place from which he fell!? This place is the land above the line and we must live there to know its nature.

It can also be hypothesized that when we <u>cease</u> to raise Cain, then we would be "raising Abel", the allegorical brother? Abel, whose voice has been crying to us from beneath the ground, may still be alive! He has just been buried under the traditions, opinions, beliefs and concepts of the fallen human nature of man who dwells below the line. What is it like above the horizontal line?!

Is anyone willing to find out in the living laboratory of his or her own body, mind and heart? Perhaps Cain and Abel are only allegorical symbols created by Moses to distinguish between the negative and the positive expressions? or the negative and positive reactions of men and women to the conditions of the material world in contrast to the **positive experience** of the connection of men and women with the world of the Spirit?

We have already alluded to the fact that fear, anger, worry, emptiness, torment and pity can be eliminated from the expression of a person and the result will be the absence of most, if not all, negative emotions from your experience. A positive emotion would replace the negative emotion as concern replaces worry. Concern and worry are not the same thing. Positive Concern is above the line and negative worry is below the line of demarcation between the clear emotions of Spirit and the polluted emotions of form.

Every positive emotion, symbolized by Abel, has its negative counterpart, symbolized by Cain. Concern/worry. Patience/impatience. Harmony/

disharmony.   Agreement/ disagreement.   Love/hate.   Comfort/ discomfort. Thankful/thankless. Happy/sad. The list can go on and on. I have placed the positive emotions first and the negative emotions second. This is done to illustrate that Abel is alive and Cain is buried beneath the ground where his voice cries out to be released into the earth.

LIVING IN THE LIGHT Above The Line is living in Heaven in your own experience; below the line is existing in the hell in your own experience.   There are people who want to continue to worry but they substitute the positive word, "concern", for the negative behavior of worry in which they are really engaged. You can't really fool your Self but your self-active human mind, the liar, the serpent, will surely try to deceive you.

Is anyone ready to say **good-bye** to the familiar Cain state of experience of the fallen state of man below the line (human nature), and **hello** to the unfamiliar and the "new" Abel state of experience above the line?Is anyone really ready to exchange the pain of the negative emotions for the comfort of the positive emotions?Is anyone really ready to let the fallen, material sense of self, the human ego, **decrease** so that the risen, spiritual sense of Self, the true ego, Man, made in the image and likeness of God, would **increase**?!We do have freedom of choice if we will use it.

A person who is willing to try to live above the line will discover that the heaviness of existing in the fallen state will become lighter in the process. Your experience of life will be different. Of course, your experience of life must be different as you replace the negative emotions of the Cain State with the positive emotions of the Abel state. The Law of Cause and Effect must work. It is the unchangeable Law of the Creator.

The problem with mankind to date has been that they did not know what to do or how to get out of the trap in which they have found themselves. They sensed that there must be a better way to live but the best advice that they could get from other people was that they are just like everybody else: **normal**. "Normal" really means "average" and "mediocre" and "only human". People innately sense that they are not mediocre.

The Truth of a person really senses that he or she is something special; that God doesn't make junk. A person has sensed this feeling of inner worth even though his or her experience has been a mixture of an Abel state and a Cain state as these two allegorical brothers fight between themselves for supremacy. The negative emotions of the Cain Indicators are so intense, so strong that the person remembers the Cain behaviors more clearly. **(It's a great warning system of wrong behavior!)**

In fact, the person uses his or her rod of God, his or her "I Am", to identify with the Cain Indicators: the person in the fallen state proudly states, I am jealous; I am angry; I am resentful; I am spiteful; I am greedy; I am the Cain Indicators. We are being warned by our discomfort when the Mark of Cain is present in our own experience. The Law works.

A person can experience a feeling but he or she is **not the feeling**. A person who has the feeling is the one who expresses the feeling in one's consciousness. A person who has freedom of choice can **choose** to express any feeling. A person can even choose to express a positive feeling. Every negative feeling (Cain Indicator) has a positive brother (Abel). Instead of being angry, a person can choose to be determined!?

Feelings can be symbolized by clouds: the **underside** of the cloud of feelings, filled with the dark negative emotions, is dark and dreary with little or no light; and the top of the cloud of feelings, filled with positive emotions, is soft and white and billowy. The top of the cloud receives and reflects the light of the Sun, a symbol for God and His radiance in our solar system. We do not omit the radiance from God from this analogy.

Any person with freedom of choice can choose to be riding on top of the white billowy cloud of feelings, or he can be underneath the cloud in the rain, snow, ice and hail. In both instances, it is the same cloud of total feelings. The person can choose the level of his or her position in the cloud of total emotions.

People who choose to remain beneath the cloud or who, uncontrollably, rise up and down in the cloud, do not know that they have a choice. Are you ready to leave the underside of the cloud where you have spent your life to date?Are you willing to say good-bye to Cain and ride on the top of the cloud?

Angels are symbolically pictured standing on the top of a cloud and playing beautiful songs on their harps. The harp is a symbol of the **physical body**. A physical body means that you are alive on earth. The strings of the harp make beautiful sounds and the beautiful sounds symbolize the positive emotions of music rather than **the noise** of the negative emotions. The problem with the familiar interpretation is that the angel playing the harp in heaven has no physical body because they have "died and gone to heaven." Are you getting the idea that you don't have to die to play your harp and make beautiful music on this side of the grave in the land Above the line.

All change must be preceded by the person's willingness to change. Are you willing to rise up to really experience that there is a land above the line? Another state is now available to you, a new state that has never been experienced by you previously. It is not really new. It has been there all along but we have been out of position and on the underside of the cloud except for an occasional leap upward where we received a very quick view of what a beautiful view that was available from a higher viewpoint.

But we always settled back down to our familiar human nature viewpoint that we inherited from our forefathers because most people are that way. The sins of the fathers have been visited upon us children. The Cain state is a sinful state. It is "**off-the-mark**". The offering by you of the Abel state is "**on the mark**". The Abel state is the Land Above The Line. Are you willing to say good-bye to the Cain state?Then, rise up out of the area of the negative emotions of the Cain state!All that you would lose is sadness, misery and gloom.

Reconsider this rearranged listing of the positive and the negative emotions. This time you should notice that the negative emotions are presented in a ***smaller italics type size***. As we look down on the negative emotions which are presented underneath the horizontal line, the land below the line, we are separating ourselves, distancing ourselves, from our past connection with them. If we can look down on them, then they are not us, they are not who We really are. They are below us. They are still there.

Consider this illustration and rearrangement of our emotions. Place yourself in the position above the Point of Observation of the Observer of your emotional realm. Affirm, **I Am the Observer**.

I Am the <u>Observer</u>

Point of Observation
****
<u>LIST OF EMOTIONS STORED IN YOUR HEART &</u>
<u>KNOWN IN YOUR MIND</u>
Positive Emotions: <u>Heavenly</u> Blessings

love	kindness	peace	appreciation	joy
fulfilled	glorious	delight	forgiveness	comfort
gladness	approval	truthful	light-hearted	worth
happiness	serenity	trust	satisfaction	resilient
confidant	ecstatic	patient	supportive	thankful
capable	willing	orderly	industrious	blessed
thrilled	repentent	creative	courage	

Living in the Light Above the Line!

Negative Emotions / Painful Blessings

hate	*guilt*	*revenge*	*resentment*	*blame*
anxiety	*grief*	*hopeless*	*dissapointed*	*worthless*
greed	*fear*	*apathy*	*resistence*	*despair*
furious	*disgust*	*insecure*	*discomfort*	*laziness*
helpless	*victimized*	*stubborn*	*frustrated*	*empty*
worried	*cursed*	*chaos*	*confusion*	*sinful*

**Learn not to choose and use your
negative emotions with your Freedom of Choice!
They will decrease in influence.
This will produce a change in your heart.**

We are in a process of ascending away from the negative emotions. The negative emotions are smaller and lower now than they were when the negative and the positive emotions were all mixed together.

As we look at our emotions from a higher vantage point, an ascended point of observation, we should begin to realize that if we can observe our negative emotions in our hearts, then they are not attached to us and a part of us. They are the negative feelings that we have and know from our past experience. They are beneath us more than they have ever been before. We can choose not to express them with our conscious mind, the director, if we so choose. **They are still lurking as fiery dragons in a cave.**

Likewise, we should begin to realize that if we can observe our **positive emotions** in our hearts, then they too are no longer a part of us. They are the positive feelings that we have and know. They are beneath us but they are closer to us than they have ever been before as they are now separated from being mixed together with the negative emotions.

If we can observe our positive emotions, then they are below us and they are closer to us. We can observe them and we can choose to express them into our world if we choose to do so with our conscious mind. They are available in our consciousness to be chosen by us when we create and express Life from ourselves into our world.

If you can see your feelings, both positive and negative, you are not your feelings. You are above your feelings and you can choose the feelings that you want to express. You can deliberately choose the positive feelings that are closer to you from your point of observation. You can continue to let the negative emotions fade further down in the distance to become smaller and smaller as you deliberately choose not to use them. You can see them more clearly as a warning system. You are thankful that there is a warning system and that you know what it is and how to use it.

You can begin to see these negative emotions positioned in the space below the horizontal line. They are further away from you and you are less likely to choose to use them because these negative emotions are the ones that give you varying degrees of discomfort. You understand that all of your emotions are your very own. You do not get **your** emotions from **other** people or conditions.

Environmental influences are **external triggers** to release your negative emotions from their subconscious lair were they have been in hiding. You will reach a point that one day you will be thankful for the external trigger that released your negative emotion so that you can discard it from the house of your Being.

Back to the analogy of the cloud. The more intense negative emotions are placed at the very bottom of the cloud that symbolizes your total emotional package. You can see them at the very bottom of the cloud which is really dark! The positive emotions are in the Light.

Your negative and your positive emotions can be seen more clearly than ever at their various levels of **discomfort** and **comfort** as you observe the total cloud, **dark and light** from your new point of observation where you can observe things more clearly. You begin to realize that you are observing your feelings from a new and a higher level of observation that is clearer than you have ever seen before in your entire experience on earth..

It is from this new vantage point of clarity, the point of observation, which is a high point in your experience to date. This point is symbolized as a dot, • , or a point from which you observe the world of your environment.You begin to sense for the first time in your life on earth that you are not this point that is at the center of your material world.

You begin to sense that you are <u>Above</u> the point **even higher** than the point, on the higher side of the point.

You begin to sense that **You** are the <u>**One**</u> who is observing your whole world. You begin to sense that **You are the <u>Observer</u>**. You begin to sense that you are ***<u>LIVING IN THE LIGHT Above The Line</u>***.

You also begin to sense that you are not here simply to **Observe** the world which you center. You begin to sense that you are here to do Something, to **create** something, because you know that you are a creator. You have created. You have created some beauty and some ugliness in the land below the line. You observe that the negative emotions were involved in the ugliness and the positive emotions were involved in your beautiful expression of Life.

It is easy from the point of the **Observer** to decide to be a **Server** of beauty. A Creator of beauty. We can sense that we objected to serving the nature of the Father in the past, but now that we are coming home we can choose to Serve the nature of the Father into the earth. We sense that the Prodigal Son in us is coming home.

We are learning to use our earthly mind and our earthly heart correctly.

Chapter 12: You Can Re-Program Your Mind And Heart

A person who is willing to say good-bye to the Cain state, the familiar human nature state of your own particular and specific experience to date, must expect to leave the past experience, which is known, as he or she moves into a new experience, which is, as yet, unknown. There will be a period of transition from the old sense of self with which you are familiar to a new sense of Self which will be a vastly different and an improved experience. I have introduced the location of the new sense of Self in the previous list of emotions as a • Point of Observation., the place of the New Self.

The area below the line has been described as filled with negative emotions that resulted from the collective judgments of the conditions in the world of your environment as seen through a **polluted** human consciousness. As far as each of us is concerned, all the activity of which we are aware is known to us because of our state of consciousness. The real activity is taking place in the material environment but we are aware of this **external** activity because of the <u>**images within**</u> **our own consciousness.** We are aware of the activity in the material environment through the use of our minds and we are aware of our feelings toward this activity through our hearts, the realm of feeling.

In our past experience in the land below the line where we have been raising Cain regularly for centuries, we have been programmed to have negative feelings about the conditions in the environment.

"How do you **feel** about this situation?" "How do you **feel** about that person?" Great emphasis has been placed upon feelings.

If we are encouraged to feel negative emotions about people, places and things and we continue to **react** in this manner to the conditions of our environment made of atoms and molecules, then we shall surely remain in the state where fear, worry, anger, resentment, hatred, jealousy, greed, etc., are acceptable and commonplace emotions in regard to our material environments.

We have blamed our negative emotions as being caused by the conditions in the environment. We should now understand that the distorted conditions in the environment are caused by the operation of the Law through our collective behavior that originates in our state of consciousness. We have been programmed to believe that our behavior is normal. After all, everybody (who lives below the line) does it!

You have been told over and over again that "You are only human, you know". If you accept that premise, there is no new and other state **above** the line for you as long as you are on earth. We have been told that the earth is a separate place that is not connected to something higher. We feel isolated and alone. We have been taught that we should just try to be "good" but it really can't be done. God and Heaven are a place that you go to **after you die**--if you don't go to that lower place. We are in a lower place now!

What is commonly taught does not fit with the teachings that **Heaven and earth are one; Spirit and form are One, the Kingdom of Heaven is at hand; Man is made in the image and likeness of God; and YOU are an immortal spirit that will go to heaven, or that other place, after you die.**

If you have an immortal spirit which is available to go to heaven when you die, then where is this eternal Spirit right now in this present moment?How can your Spirit <u>go</u> to heaven when you die unless it is <u>here</u> on earth right now?!The Spirit must be <u>here</u> before it can go <u>there</u>!You should begin to understand that Your Spirit is in Your Form.

Are you the eternal spirit, or are you the earthly container that has been made of the dust of the ground called atoms and molecules? **Which are you: spirit or form?**Who are you: the spirit that survives? or, the form that disintegrates?So far, no one has been able to prove it one way or another while they remain in the land below the line raising Cain.. There is another higher state available to us which is **above the line** on this side of the grave. You have been invited to rise up in consciousness to experience this place where your Cosmic Self resides.

You have freedom of choice! You can use your ability to choose to stop reacting to the material patterns in your environment that were perfectly modeled after the patterns in your consciousness and the mass consciousness. Are you willing to say good-bye to Cain?Can you choose to stop reacting to the patterns of form that exist in the material world that are made through the mass consciousness?Can you take another look and see, objectively, without negative emotions, the **images in your consciousness** of the actual things in your environment as they really are? They are perfectly what they are and they were made by the operation of the Law!

The earthly creature, who is "only human", can't, or rather **won't use the freedom of choice** to say good-bye to raising Cain and this fallen creature will continue to create the conditions of the land below the line. However, the Truth of Man, the Spirit made in the image and likeness of God, which is also present, can say good-bye to the land below the line because your True Spirit does not raise Cain. **YOU** are not Cain. The real **YOU**, the spirit that inhabits the form, has allowed the counterfeit self to act the role of Cain for such a long time that people believe that they are Cain, that they are "only human".

People in the fallen state sincerely believe that there is no other state. They freely admit that they are in a fallen state but they either have no awareness or they deny that there is a higher state from which they fell, and that this higher state is available on this side of the grave. They do this because they are unwilling to change or they don't know. It is really very easy to forgive people who do not know. People who are unwilling to change will suffer the effects of the Law which is always in operation.

They also believe that if you want to experience this other state, you have to die in order for your spirit to get "there". They also sincerely believe that Death, the absence of Life from their human form, is the price of entrance to the higher realm. But your spirit is already here or you wouldn't be alive. Life is an attribute or a property of spirit. **YOU** are a spirit and **YOU** are alive. Life is everlasting and eternal. The nature of life is to be alive. The nature of life is to live. Life doesn't die. "Dead" life is a contradiction in terms.

Life lives in forms, human and otherwise. The presence of Life in the land below the line is aware of the negative emotions which have been generated as the **distortions** of life, that have been created by the misuse of life to create distorted material forms. The power of Life has been usurped by the false self, the counterfeit self, and the power has been used to create conditions, lies, negative emotions and distorted forms that we have called "normal" in the land below the line, the distorted world of turmoil in which we live.

Life could also have been used to generate the forms and conditions, and the positive emotions that are inherent and truly natural to the design of life. Life can't do both at the same time. If the counterfeit and distorted state has been generated on earth for a certain period of time, then the true state can not have been generated during that same time period. What we have in our material world is a mixture of the true and the counterfeit depending upon what mankind has created through the individual human consciousness. The Law Works!

Each person is connected directly to the Source of life which is coming through you in every moment. **YOU** are alive! A single person can choose to say good-bye to the fallen state and begin to express the truth of life instead of the counterfeit state using the negative emotions to create distortions, chaos and turmoil. If a single person actually does this, then a new state, a true state, would be present on earth for others to observe. That person would be visible point of orientation, •, a **True example,** for others to see.

Any person who would choose to leave the lower state and successfully accomplishes the feat would know **two** different states: he would know the fallen state and he would also know the new state as he (or she) creates it. He could then be positioned in the new state and call out to his friends in the lower state to leave that state of distortion and return to the true state that is not distorted. Come up here. Come up hither! Come unto me! A person who **knows** the way is in position to **show** the Way. Rise up my love , my fair one, and come away with me to the land above the line where the LIGHT shines constantly.

Each Spirit, each person, can only generate a true state through and around themselves, through and around the equipment of their own heart, mind and body. In order for any person to experience the new state, that person would have to generate the new state in daily and momentary living. The existence of the true state may have been **proved** by some other person in the past, but it must be **reproved** by one's self in the present. Then the person who did it would know, really know, because he had generated the true state in one's own experience and he could observe the new world of his own creation.

The evidence of the spirit of **Life**, which is present in everyone, contains the spirit of **Love**, which is the Power, and the spirit of **Truth**, which contains the design, from the Intelligent Creator. These three spirits are intertwined and as inseparable as braided threads. The human form of body, mind and heart is designed to reveal the triune nature of these three intertwined spirits. The spirit of Love is to flow through the heart; the spirit of Truth is to flow through the mind; and the spirit of Life is to flow through the human body in momentary living.

In the true state, the spirits of Love, Truth and Life would flow through the heart, mind and body of the person who is willing to let it be so. This is not the old, fallen, lower, "raising Cain" state. It is a new state that is known by the person who creates the new state in his or her own experience. The old experience of the fallen state will be replaced by the new experience of the true state, a higher state which would accurately resemble the original state intended by the Intelligent Designer.(We could label it the True State, the Abel state, or the Seth state for those familiar with the terminology of the Book of *Genesis* in the Old Testament.)

The triune spirit of Love, Truth and Life is also known as the **Shekinah** in the Old Testament and the **Christ** spirit in the New Testament. This state is above the Abel state

because it is the pure undistorted radiance from God, the Father, Allah. The person who generates this spirit of Love, Truth and Life through their earthly equipment, regardless of their beliefs, would know the experience of being a Son of the Covenant, or a Christian, or a Muslim who have totally devoted themselves to Allah, the Arabic name for God. A person, male or female, who receives and transmits the **radiance** from God, the spirit of Love Truth and Life, through the heart, mind and body would know the experience and the meaning of the Star of David. *(See the graphic of the Star of David or Solomon's Seal)*

FATHER SPIRIT
(Upper Triangle of <u>Spirit</u>)

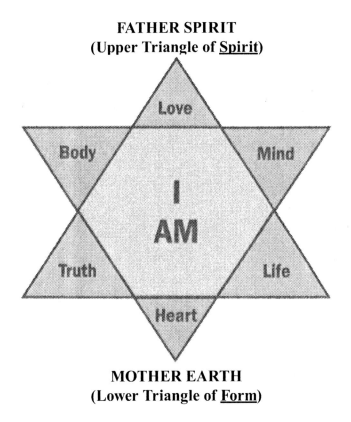

MOTHER EARTH
(Lower Triangle of <u>Form</u>)

This symbol of the Star of David is an accurate illustration of your True Self. Your physical body with its mind and heart were made from the dust of the ground, from Mother Earth.

The Radiance from God. which is the triune Spirit of Love, Truth and Life that comes from God, and also known as the Shekinah and the Christ Radiance, is allowed to be received by the heart, mind and body.

Your individual Spirit, I Am, is in the keystone in the center of the Star and your True Self receives the input from the Spirit that is coming directly to you come through you. When this occurs, everything is on automatic.

The transitional change of experience from the lower state of consciousness is the Path to a higher state of consciousness. It is a transitional experience.The transition can be visually demonstrated by using the example of a glass of **muddy** water to symbolize the contents of the mind and the heart, the consciousness of the fallen human state. The challenge is to replace the muddy water in the glass with clear water **without emptying the glass and filling it with clean water**. You are not allowed to discard the muddy water in the glass because the glass represents the present condition of your consciousness and you cannot throw away the past experiences of your life. Some people believe that the task is impossible. If they continue to believe this, they won't try the following answer.

It is very easy to demonstrate that the muddy water can be replaced with clear water without emptying the glass. You do this by holding the glass filled with muddy water under a faucet of flowing **clean water** and observe the muddy water become less muddy and more clear as clean water is allowed to flow into the container which held the muddy water. You can visualize the transitional experience.

You can observe the operation of the Law. If you understand the simple example with regard to the glass of polluted water that became clean, you can see the application for cleaning your heart and mind by allowing the Spirit of Love, Truth and Life to freely flow. **Water is the earthly symbol of Truth**. **Your consciousness can be cleaned in this manner.**

The theory is simple. Let the nature of spirit--a nature of love, truth and life, which is the true nature of Man coming from God--flow into the equipment of the heart, mind and body of the person and the replacement of the polluted consciousness with clean consciousness is certain and inevitable for those who hold true to the creative process. The Law works!

Of course, you are not allowed to add mud from the ground to the clean water in the glass which would be the re-introduction of the corruption from the fallen state. Any relapses mean that you must begin again. If you fall, you must begin again. Everyone in the fallen state has a muddy consciousness so we are not alone. The goal is to remain in the flow in the present moment.

You do not have to make the Flow. It is present and it is always flowing. Remember that all water is clean and clear water. Muddy water is clean water with dirt from the earth **suspended** in it or **dissolved** in it. The Truth of **YOU** is a clean consciousness. The dirt in the muddy water is a symbol of the content of the earthly state of consciousness in the fallen state. There is nothing wrong with having a muddy consciousness. **A muddy and polluted condition is the starting point for <u>everyone</u>.** Welcome to the club! The problem is in the **pollution** within the consciousness. Pollution can be cleaned if we are willing and if we choose to let it pass away. The Law works.

A person with a polluted consciousness has this condition because they observe the conditions of their particular environment and continue to generate negative emotions and negative **<u>reactions</u>** with respect to the conditions in the environment, which are perfectly producing the things in the consciousness They continue to believe that the polluted environment can be "fixed". There is nothing wrong with the conditions in the environment. The Law produced them! The Source of the problem is the human consciousness.

The process of cleansing the consciousness, purifying the heart, requires that a person cease reacting to the distorted forms in the environment to produce more negative emotions which will predictably muddy the waters of consciousness even more.

Why react to the distortions in your environment which are **"perfect" distortions in material forms. What was sown from consciousness is reaped exactly and absolutely**. The Divine Law of Sowing and Reaping works perfectly. If people make war, they reap war. If people are peaceful, they reap peace. The law is very, very exact. The behaviors of people and the forms in the environment have been sown by mankind which has been in the fallen state for a long, long time. Material conditions can be no other way unless they are changed in consciousness **first**.

If we want a beautiful environment, then we must express beauty. Negative emotions are not beautiful. Negative emotions are **Painful Blessings** to remind you when **you are WRONG.** They were designed to inform and warn the person who experienced them that the wrong feelings were used to produce wrong behaviors to produce a distorted world. **The human body with its mind and heart is an intelligent design, a Divine Design, created by an Intelligent Designer.**

It is possible for a counterfeit person, who is willing, to change his expression from the lower state to the higher and new and true expression of **the indwelling spirit**. **YOU** are the indwelling spirit. In order to begin this divine drama, we must act the role of Who we really are. The fact of the matter is that we have been acting the role of who we are **not**--a false self, who is "only human, you know", and who has all these faults that we don't want to let go of. So, how can they pass away if we don't let go! It'll never happen!

An individual in the fallen state must choose to change and express the True Nature of Spirit, which is what we truly are. Just as an individual is the unit of society in the fallen state, a person of Spirit is the individual cell of an individual Being in the body of God on earth in a variety of human forms, male and female. The Spirit is in the Form.

God's spirit, which is **everywhere**, is also in the body of mankind. Our responsibility is to let the Spirit from God, our individual focus of Spirit, flow from us into the earth so that the kingdom of the spirit will come on earth in material forms. This is the purpose for the human forms of man. Man is the connecting link between Spirit and form. We have been the missing link.

God's spirit has always been flowing continuously and unceasingly through the body of mankind in every generationMankind, generally, has not been aware of the invisible flow of the spirit of God because we have **ignored** the Spirit from God which made us **ignorant,** instead of **wise**. The Law worked! We have usurped the Power from God and used it to make the muddy generation of the land below the line. This has been and is an evil generation!

It is time for those with ears to hear to generate the pure water of the Truth of Love in our individual creative fields in our momentary living. Let it be so in our experience. Let us begin.

Let the spirit that is coming directly to you from God come through you and you will generate the conditions of the Land Above the Line through a clean heart and a creative mind. You will be working in the Garden from which our ancestors fell and you will be ***LIVING IN THE LIGHT Above The Line.***

Remember. Your True Starting Point is not your fallen human nature which is the land of turmoil, and chaos below the line. Your starting point is in your Spiritual Identity. You are a **Spiritual Being**. You have use of a human form on a temporary basis.

Let the Spirit that you are radiate through your human equipment.

Chapter 13: Let Spirit Radiate From You

We can begin to understand the value of a clean, clear consciousness to perceive our environment correctly. A clean consciousness is symbolized by the crystal clear "water" of the Spirit of Truth. The Spirit of Truth flows from the Creator into the individual consciousness to take form in the visible earth. God sends only the purity of crystal clear water. God has no pollution to send to us.

All of the distorted conditions on earth are produced and re-produced in the consciousness, the mind and heart, of mankind in the fallen state. The muddy and murky distortions in the material world originate in the muddy and murky depths of the polluted hearts of men and women. This pollution in the material forms of the earth is what we have created. We usurped God's power to do this.

All of our attempts to "fix" the "bad" conditions in the material environment are simply efforts of moving the distorted forms, the ugly furniture we created, from one place to another in the fallen material world. The problem is that the furniture in the big room of planet Earth is the wrong furniture. The forms in the environment need to be replaced with new forms made using the Clear Spirit that is constantly coming to us. Human beings have created the material world through the discord that exists within ourselves, our families, our homes and between nations.The **discord** is the direct result of our negative expressions from our consciousness.

Beings in human forms can also make the **accord** and the agreement utilizing the positive expressions which would result in a harmonious environment. Nothing else has worked over millennia. As an individual creator, we are only responsible for the "ugly furniture" that we make and place into the world. There is a real need for beautiful "furniture" to be created in the material world. God made Earth a place for beauty to be born through us.

The new **spirit** must be put into new **forms** by using the crystal, clean spirit symbolized by the crystal clean **water** of Truth. that comes directly to us from the **Intelligent Designer.** There is no intermediate connection between you and God. We never have to pray to God to send His Radiance to us. God's Radiance has already been sent and the beauty and design of the Perfect World is available to be received by those who will receive it.

If there is to be prayer by mankind, it would be for us to open our hearts to receive what has always been sent in the past, what will be sent in the future, and what is being sent to us in the present moment. As we receive this pure Radiance, we let it be pressed through our individual consciousness to produce the new **"wine"** of Love, Truth and Life that has come into the world through our hearts, minds and bodies. This new **"wine of Life"** must be put into new **bottles,** new forms, new "furniture" in the material world.

You should understand that the New wine is **never** made by using the grapes of wrath (the negative emotions which are the painful blessings). New Wine is made by utilizing the beautiful positive emotions to create beautiful conditions. This beautiful condition on Earth was also described by Moses as the Garden of Eden before the fall of man when **people lived Above the Line** in agreement with the Spirit from God that flowed **to** the Children of God and **through** them into the material world.

It is also the condition known in the New Testament as the expression of the One Spirit where people are living and being with **one accord in one <u>place</u> expressing the Christ Spirit, the spirit of Love,. Truth and Life**. The planet Earth, exactly where **YOU** are, is the place. The Edenic state is created through a consciousness which is clean and clear. It is clean and clear because the love from God to the creation of Man is received and passed on to the forms created on earth during a period of time known as the **Golden Age of Man, the original condition of Man.** The Golden Age is not in form now. The experience of Man has descended from the Golden Age, to the Silver Age, to the Bronze Age to the present Iron Age.

Gold is an earthly symbol of Love because the metal Gold never changes, **never tarnishes**. It can be drawn into fine wire, molded into any shape, it can be beaten into foil and it is an excellent conductor of electricity with minimum resistance. Gold doesn't change no matter what you physically do to it. It does not tarnish, as does **silver**, due to reaction with influences from the environment that produces pollution, the blackness or the dross on the silver. This should give us a better idea of the **Silver Age of Man** that was a bit lower than the Golden Age. The Silver Age was lower than the Golden Age as the fall of man continued. The descent gets even worse as mankind tuned out God.

As man continued in his separation from the impulse of the Radiance of Spirit that was coming to him, his fall became even more noticeable to him and he tried to recreate the Golden Age from which he had fallen. In his ignorance (he continued to ignore the Love and Truth in Spirit from the Creator), he tries to re-create the Golden Age without any dependence upon or spiritual input from God. Man tried to use his creative power to build a golden age, which he senses is possible, but the best that he could do, without God, was to create a shiny new world that had an appearance of Gold. This was the introduction of the **Brass Age of Man**. The created things of this material world, like brass, soon began to tarnish and lose its artificial luster. Man descended even further into the fallen state of separation from True Source. Man is moving but he is moving in the wrong direction: down instead of up.

The conditions in man's consciousness and in the conditions in the material world that reflects man's consciousness continues to decay and become even worse. We are now living in a world of decay and death. We are living in the **Iron Age of Man**. We are as low as we can get and we are in the fallen state because mankind is in a fallen state. Iron has great strength but when it is exposed to the environment, it begins to rust and decay. It is only a matter of time until the once-strong metal falls apart as the iron rust weakens the iron. It inevitably falls to the ground.

This Iron Age is seen for its decadence and decay as it continues to crumble from within. It is doomed to failure because Man has moved in the wrong direction as his consciousness has become increasingly more polluted. Is there no hope for Man in the Iron Age?! Yes. There is another direction and it is upward. It is the return to the direction from which man fell. It is the return of individuals who are brave and willing enough to admit past mistakes and begin the return to the land above the horizontal line and **LIVING IN THE LIGHT** <u>**Above The Line**</u>. **This is the opportunity for Man to return to the Golden Age before Man destroys himself.**

During this downward transitional fall from grace, God has never ceased to send His Love, His Truth and His Life to His people on earth. The very act of people praying to God to send blessings to the earth is based in the false premise that **God Almighty is not doing His job**. This is the blasphemy. God always sends His perfect radiance to mankind. God always honors His Law. The problem has been that the consciousness of fallen people has distorted the impulse of the perfect radiance from God to produce distorted and grotesque man-made forms. Then, seeing the distorted forms, we decided that we didn't like them so we decided to "improve" the world with "better" distorted forms of our own creation--without the design from the Creator.

What we created in our fallen state that we sincerely thought would be more beneficial to us, produced the downward journey from the **Golden Age**, to the **Silver Age**, to the **Brass Age** to this **Iron Age**. During the downward spiral, we allowed selfishness and greed for the material things in the environment to enter into the creation. We had no need for the heavenly treasure from God in heaven; the fallen person wanted the treasures from the earth for himself--**without any help from God**.

The clear consciousness became muddy with its ever increasing desires for treasures from the earth. The mud was added from the earth, which is the only source of mud. The consciousness of Man fell from the heaven into the earth, from the **land Above the Line** to the land below the line. The muddy state of consciousness has become the "norm" for the inhabitants of the earth in this disintegrating Iron Age. **The Iron Age is strong but it is disintegrating. Do not be fooled by the appearance of material things that indicate progress.**

Powerful weapons are available for mankind to destroy itself by the dark forces of disharmony and hatred. New technologies are being used by factions of people with deeply embedded beliefs to fight political wars, religious wars, scientific wars, wars of fallen man against his environment that endangers Spaceship Earth and its inhabitants.

As long as we are living in this disintegrating Iron Age, which are the conditions of the land below the line, we are in danger. The counterfeit and unreal selves, who are "only human", who occupy the land below the line and who create polluted conditions from a polluted state of consciousness, are **self destructive**.

The false self and the distorted world that it creates cannot continue indefinitely. It has already disintegrated from the Golden Age, to the Silver Age, to the Brass Age to this Iron Age. In fact, the Iron Age is doomed for elimination by its own pollution. The only answer is the dissolution of the false self and the replacement of it with the True Self, the Divine Self in one generation of time. This new Self is the only Way to bring the Golden Age into manifestation.

If there are those people on earth who choose *LIVING IN THE LIGHT Above The Line, then, they will create the Kingdom as surely as the false world disintegrates in their own experience. The Law works.* **This creative process can either be viewed as**

a Blessing or a Warning. If you ascend to LIVING IN THE LIGHT <u>Above the Line</u>, you will be <u>Blessed</u>.

If not, you have been <u>warned</u> and You shall experience the evidence of the **absence of Love** in action on Earth in the land below the line which is only temporary. Once more, the Children of Men have been given the opportunity to create the True Kingdom on Earth.

Prophets, Teachers and Gurus, who have advocated the message of a return to the clean state of consciousness, a return to the pure in heart which will return the Edenic state to the earth, have been ignored. The people who have become so familiar with raising Cain, which has been making them miserable, do not want to change! How intelligent is that!? Yet, they say that they want peace on earth and they pray for God to send the peace that they do not have, all the while ignoring the **perfect peace** which is being radiated to them and ignored by them.

As people willingly relinquish and move away from this polluted, lower state, they discover that there are many positive emotions and expressions from which to choose to be creative. No matter how terrible the conditions and the distortions in the environment happen to be, a person can always be thankful with his heart that the information which the mind is bringing from the distorted environment is a true image of the **perfect distorted conditions** that were made by the Law. We can always be thankful that the Law is in operation. Thankfulness is a positive emotion that can be used to build the Real Kingdom, the return of the **Golden Age**. Certainly, complaint won't do it.

Even if the information conveyed from the fallen state is polluted and as a junkyard, that's exactly what we made by our expressions: We have and we are creating the rusty and decaying Iron Age of Man. It is good to see exactly what we have made rather than remain **blind** to our personal role in the fall of man in this day and age. If we acknowledge that we have been blind in the past, then we are in a position where we can begin to see clearly in the present. Our perceptual blindness has been healed.

An honest person can appreciate the exactness of the operation of the Law of Sowing and Reaping: it is good to know that if we plant weed seeds, we get weeds; it is comforting to know that if people sow the True Seed, the results will reflect very accurately the effect of the Good Seed which is sown.

A person can be patient and understanding that not one jot or one tittle shall escape the working of the Law. Garbage in; garbage out produces the fallen state: **RUST!** Heaven in; heaven out produces the Divine State: **The GOLDEN AGE!.** The keys to the Kingdom are people who are ***LIVING IN THE LIGHT Above The Line.***

A person can be extremely confident that any creation from the **heaven** of one's consciousness will surely and absolutely be duplicated **in form** on the earth. The earth cannot refuse to accept the expression that is released from the consciousness of man. This is a part of the Divine Order and the Divine Design. The Spirit that is coming to you from God must come through you without distortion, or you get the land below the line. The choice is yours.

But man has been so busy trying to change the distorted forms of what has been expressed in the past through the polluted consciousness of the body of mankind without any success, that he has not seen the simple solution of changing the nature of what individual man is expressing into the environment in the present moment. God forgives us this error which has punished us based on the nature of what we expressed. We created our own punishment for our rebellion from the LORD, the Father, God, Allah.

God is forgiving. Man is forgiving. Man is also **for giving**. Mankind, Man, male and female, was created by God as an instrument for **giving the blessings from God into the earth.** Man was not created to **get** material treasures from the earth to accumulate and store them for his own selfish purposes. Well intentioned people sincerely pray to God to let **"Thy will be done"**, but, they really function in such a manner to let **"my will be done"**. **And the Law works!** We have reaped what we sowed. Gold to Silver to Brass to Iron. Have we had enough of this stupidity, the usurpation of God's power, the painful

110

blessings we bring upon ourselves, the predictable deterioration and death?! Are we willing to change, or to go down the drain?!

The material circumstances on earth reflect, **exactly,** the condition that exists in the consciousness of mankind—as it should and as it must. **The Law works!** The selfish desires of fallen man have replaced the blessings from God through man. Man in the fallen state has stolen the "fire", the power, the design and the life from God, and used it for his own purposes, his own selfish and self-centered, polluted designs.

The earth is the LORD's and thus, fallen man has become a thief. It is easy to understand the statement that the earth, which should be a house of prayer, a house where the positive emotions and beautiful forms should be everywhere, has become a den of thieves.

The transition of an individual from a thief, who takes and uses the LORD's power for himself, to one who prays, one who **serves** the LORD's spirit of Love, Truth and Life into the earth of the material world, is what is meant by **repentance**. True Repentance is absolutely necessary before the kingdom of heaven from God puts in an appearance on earth.

Each person has an individual responsibility directly to God because the spiritual connection between the individual human form and the spirit of God is **a direct connection**. The responsibility of each person is to let the spirit from God radiate through the individual heart, mind and body into the earth where the physical forms on earth will reveal the Spirit which was used to build the forms. Isn't that a simple system!?

All the prophets of God did their best to refer everyone to the LORD, the Father or Allah. It is an evasion of individual responsibility to look to others to do their parts and to complain about the situation because others are not doing what they are supposed to do. We should do what we are supposed it do. If others don't do their part, the Law will work through them without our help to produce the distorted conditions that we deserve.

The First Commandment, <u>and it is a **command** not a suggestion,</u> is **I AM THE LORD THY GOD; THOU SHALL NOT HAVE STRANGE GODS BEFORE ME**. The strange gods are the distorted **material forms** of the earth. The command has also been phrased that an individual should love the LORD Thy God with **all** thy heart, and **all** thy mind and all thy soul (the physical form) and **all** thy strength. The definition of **all** is **100%**.

This is the only way that the Kingdom of Heaven will be brought to earth. There is nothing wrong with the material forms of the earth. Material forms are perfect replicas of the images that are in the consciousness. The only problem is if you love the material forms **more** than you love the **Spirit that is coming to you from God**.

The spirit of God within the heart, mind and body of a person on earth will hear the command and begin to pray without ceasing. **The simple prayer is to Let the spirit from God that is coming to you flow through you.** This is repentance. The true prayer is to let the spirit of love, truth and life from God come into the world on a moment by moment basis. It is not telling God over and over again what you want from Him to make **you** happy on earth. God is not our genie who serves us! We serve God by serving His Spirit into the earth. This voluntary act on your part immediately reintroduces you and includes you in God's world that mankind rejected and ignored years ago.

If only one person ceases to infect the world by eliminating the Mark of Cain from himself or herself, then that expression will be reflected on earth because the Law works. Perhaps someone else will notice what that one person will be doing and decide to **join** in the elimination of the fallen state through people. **<u>Perhaps they won't even notice!</u>**

<u>So what</u> if they don't! The only important question is, **<u>What will I do?</u>**

Our responsibility is to God. If we wait for everybody to change before we change, (which is a common thought that indicates great resistance) then, we will be among the last rather than among the first in keeping the First Commandment..

It is an individual choice.Do you really think that **everybody** who were around Moses, Israel, David, Solomon, Isaiah, Jesus, John, Buddha, Mohammed, Lao Tzu, Baha'u'llah, Nanak, etc. heard the message that these men delivered and that they actually repented!? (Moses spent 40 years in the wilderness with his stiff-necked people who refused to change.)

Each person must come to repentance individually. Even God the Father, Allah, cannot and will not **force** His Radiance to manifest through the heart, mind and body of any individual to bring the True Design. God gave us freedom to choose. He will not take it away. He will not force His will on Man. He will not remove the operation of the Law, His Law, for our salvation and blessing while we ignore Him. The Children of God must offer to serve their Father.

The person who lets God's spirit manifest on earth <u>**instantly**</u> receives love, truth and life as he releases this spirit into the world. The person will thus know the **heavenly fire** of Spirit that falls from Heaven; the person who doesn't let God's spirit manifest on earth, receives distortions and death, the **hell fire of the land below the line.** In both cases, the fire falls from heaven to produce either beauty or chaos through you.Isn't that fair!?

The power of God moving through a person is like a current of electricity moving through a metallic wire: if the wire is **thick**, the resistance is **high** and the metal will generate <u>**heat**</u>; but, if the wire is **fine**, and the resistance is **low,** then the metal will generate <u>**light**</u>. Same electricity, symbolizing the power from God; same "metal", symbolizing the human form; different resistances, symbolizing the unwillingness or the willingness to repent and let the current flow; different results in the human "wires" that produce either heat or light. What is your experience!? It should reveal the amount of your resistance to you.

Light symbolizes the person who knows the light from God by being a fine person who serves God's Spirit into the world. Heat symbolizes the coarse and thick person being burned by resisting the power. It is all God's power. There is no other power. The Light or heat is the result of an individual choice to **<u>Live Above the Line</u>** or <u>die below the line</u>. You are choosing Life or death. You can choose to let the Spirit radiate from you, or not.

The result of your choice will be LIGHT, or Heat. Your conscious mind will know what you express.

We recommend that your choice should be ***<u>LIVING IN THE LIGHT Above The Line.</u>***

We recommend that you **Stop Dying and Start Living**.

Chapter 14: You Know
What You Express

A person always knows with their conscious mind what he or she expresses from themselves. If a person expresses the negative emotions of anger, greed, fear, emptiness, self-pity, torment, etc, then the mind of that person knows the experience of those negative emotions because the person expressed them. If you play a negative song on your bodily equipment, you know that negative experience. Conversely, if you play the positive spirits of love, truth and life, which are the radiance from God, your experience will be lovely, truthful and full of life.

As you deliberately choose what "music" you will play on the harp of your body, then you will be in control of your experience regardless of your material environment or the people around you. You have the freedom to choose for yourself this day whether you will serve God, or mammon: the Radiance from God; or, the external influences which are the peer pressure from the environment of the polluted world that has been made by the consciousness of man in the fallen state of the Iron Age..

You do not get **your feelings** from the molecules that compose the forms in the environment. You get your feelings from your own heart and your own expression. The source of your feelings is your own heart and mind. Feelings are an "inside job" even though we are in the habit of blaming or assigning to other people the feelings that we experience internally.

 Let us consider two examples utilizing the familiar feelings of fear and love. You have probably had the experience of thinking that you were all alone in a room, turned around and suddenly noticed another person that you did not expect to see standing there. A feeling of fear ran through your body. Your words were, **"Oh! <u>You</u> scared me!"**

This feeling of fear occurred only in your body, with its heart and mind. The person whom you blamed as the "cause" of your fear did not have the feeling of fear that you experienced. He probably wondered why you had the reaction that you did because he was happy and pleased to see you standing there.

Why were there two such different feelings, fear and love, in the two people A mind in the fallen state **will accuse** someone else of making the negative feeling experienced within their own body. Beware of the accuser (your counterfeit self) when you accuse another person **outside** of you for making your **internal** feeling. Your feelings are always **your** feelings.

Here is a great illustration that changed my entire experience of Life when I first heard it from a friend. I applied the message to myself and discovered that it was true. The illustration uses the example of love between a man and a woman, specifically between me and the woman who became my wife.

My friend,(to whom I have dedicated this book) taught me that a very common mistake is made by a man who has never before experienced the intense feeling of love, until he meets the "special" love of his life. Since the person who has the intense feeling of love has never before experienced such an intense feeling until he met this woman, he believes that he obtained the feeling of love **<u>from</u> <u>her</u>**. After all, he never had such an intense feeling until he met her.

The man in this example does not really realize that he has the intense feeling of love because he **expressed love** to her and, consequently, he knows what he expressed. The woman was not the **source** of his feeling of love. **She was the object of his affection. The love experience was his own internal experience and the feeling did not come from her.** This simple example of the truth was a revelation to me! This was my very first indication that I could radiate Love, the Spirit of Love, to an object in the environment and generate an intense feeling of love in myself. **The source and the control are in me.**

On the other hand, if she has a similar feeling of love, then it was because she expressed love to me. **I was the object of her affection.** Both of us were in agreement with our mutual expression of love toward the other. Her specific feeling of love that was known in her body was **her** own expression which produced **her** experience. Each person's feelings are their own. In this example, both of the parties believed **incorrectly** that they have received the feeling of love **from** the other person. Why is this so important?!

It is possible for two people love each other, get married and after several years, the man "feels" that his wife doesn't love him any more. He comes to this conclusion because he doesn't have the **feeling** of love in the present that he had when he first met her. Since he thought, incorrectly, that his feeling of love originally **came from** the woman that he married. Now that he no longer has that feeling of love, then, **the problem must be with her**. But the problem isn't in her at all!

After all, he rationalizes incorrectly, that he got the feeling of love from her in the first place, that she was responsible for making his feeling, but now, he doesn't have the feeling of love any longer, then the problem must be with her. She is not **giving him** the feeling of love any longer. **What's wrong with her?!**

She could be loving him more than ever, generating beautiful feelings of love within herself toward him, because she knows what she expresses and she is totally unaware of **his** absence of feeling, his **lack** of love that he himself **has caused** because he is not loving her. He does not know that the reason that he is not **feeling** love any more is because he **stopped expressing love toward her, the <u>object</u> of his affection**.

When he stopped expressing love toward his wife, his feeling of love "goes away". It goes away because he is not generating and expressing the feeling anymore. Then, he sees someone else and begins to radiate love in a new direction toward the new person, and he mistakenly thinks, once again, that he is **<u>getting</u>** love from the new woman. But, the fact is that he is really generating it himself. He is giving the credit to the new woman for the new love that he is feeling. People who stop loving cease to feel love. **You know what you express**.

The man did not know that the feeling of love is an "inside job". He was the one who stopped loving, stopped making the feeling and then he blamed his wife for his lack of the expression and the experience of love. He mistakenly thinks that he can get love from a new external source. What he did find was another object of his affection and he gave the new woman credit for a feeling that he made within himself. His feelings are his own. He will probably repeat his mistake because he doesn't know that **You know what you express.**

Here are other examples of blaming someone or something else for your own feelings. You can choose to hate your job and blame the job for your lousy feeling while you are the one who generated the hatred and experience the negative feelings stored in your own heart.

You could be disgusted with the performance of "your" football team and not know that you generate the disgust. You blame the team you know only from a television tube for making your negative emotions. You blame the car in front of you for your feeling of impatience or your feeling of anger or road rage.

People in the fallen state are in the habit of believing very sincerely that their feelings are made by things and conditions in the external environment and they blame the objects made of atoms and molecules for creating their feelings. Is this dumb!? Your feelings, positive or negative, by definition, are always **your** feelings. The negative emotions are evidence of an impure, polluted heart. The negative emotions which seem so "bad" are not seen as the warning signs, and the "Painful Blessings" that can be used to cleanse the heart of impurities.

Can we begin to understand the reason why a woman stays with a drunken husband? If she **loves** him, she feels the love that she is expressing toward him regardless of his faults and his behaviors. She knows the feelings that she expresses. He is the <u>object</u> of <u>her</u> affection! Likewise, a man who love's his wife, regardless of what she does, is the one who is generating the love. He knows what he expresses.

A person can choose to express a positive emotion into a job when conditions at work aren't going the way that he would like for them to be; he can be **thankful** that he sees clearly the way things are. He is generating thankfulness and he knows what he expresses.

The Law works. You know what you express and you reap what you sow. Why hate your job!? It's your hate and your experience! There is a better way. Choose a positive feeling as long as you are in the job, and choose when to change your job.

The purpose of these examples is to help those who want to be helped to realize that all of their feelings are **their own feelings**. They are generated by and within themselves. Feelings are an inside job, always. No one else makes you mad; that is your own anger which comes from your heart when it is triggered by an external condition or event. A person who truly accepts the responsibility for his or her own emotions has the opportunity to be aware of the negative emotions stored deep within their hearts as they rise to the surface of the conscious mind.

You can deal with the negative emotion as it is released from the subconscious heart, if you choose to acknowledge the internal source. You can trample out the vintage where the grapes of wrath are stored--within yourself and, specifically, within your own heart. What will you replace the negative emotion with!?

The creative flow! You do not have to create God, the Radiance from God, the flow from the Source. All that you need to do is receive what is being sent from the Intelligent Designer and express that into the world of your environment. Then let the Law work. It is exciting and a joy to see the power of Spiritual Expression at work.

People have the opportunity to choose to let the spirits of love, truth and life radiate through them in their own experience. People can also choose to ignore the radiance and experience the dark side of the moving force. The choice is yours!

The opening of your heart can be opened either **vertically**, to the spiritual source, or, **horizontally**, to the influences from the material world. The Law will work and reveal your choice to you in **beautiful blessings** or **painful blessings. Both are yours.**

You can choose to let love and the differentiations of love radiate forth and enjoy ***LIVING IN THE LIGHT Above The Line*** as long as you are in a physical body, or you can choose to remain in the painful land below the line and continue to blame others for all your emotional pains.

You can leave the land of the dying and enjoy the land of the living. The **Spirit** of God Almighty is more powerful than the world of atoms and molecules, which is only **stuff**.

Negative emotions as they are expressed through you are the evidence that you are on the downward path that leads to dying and death. The expression of positive emotions are the evidence that You are on the upward path to living and Life.

It is time for people with integrity to **stop dying and start living**. It is time to be Who you really are, The Real Self, the real Spiritual Being within a human form, the Real I Am.

My mentor summarized the process beautifully when he wrote this poem that I have kept on my desk for more than 30 years. It is still there today.

Any Moment

Any moment of hating,
Any moment of lying,
Any moment of resentment,
Is a moment of dying.

Any moment of loving,
Any moment of giving,
Any moment of thankfulness,
Is a moment of living.

All our moments add together,
Like the digits in a sum,
And the answer tells us plainly,
Whether life or death shall come.

Martin Cecil

This simple poem conveys the Truth of the operation of the Law of Sowing and Reaping and advises each of us to monitor our **moments** in living. It teaches us that we shall know immediately what we express. If we express hatred, lies and resentment, we shall know, in that very moment, what we have expressed. It teaches us that we are not punished for our wrong behavior, or sin, at some later time after death; we are punished in the moment by our wrong expression of the True Spirit that is coming to us. This is the sin. It implies that our sins are known by our negative emotions and feelings which are our own.

If we **choose** to express love, giving generously of our positive emotions to others, and being thankful, then, in that very moment, our conscious mind knows what we have expressed. In the moment of right expression, we are rewarded by our virtue. One choice, and we do have freedom to choose, is an experience of dying; and the other choice is an experience of living.

But do we really have a choice if we desire to avoid the punishment of being burned by our own choices and our own behaviors!? Punishment from wrong expression, from sin, is like the Mark of Cain--it was designed by God and built into the system to **protect** us. The little poem teaches us that we do have a choice.

If we take an honest look at the nature of our momentary expressions, we can understand, with mathematical certainty, that we are the author of our own experience, and we have the potential to master our expression with some practice. But we must practice! We can't learn to play a musical instrument without practice. Neither can we learn to play the human instrument of heart, mind and body without practice.

And if we do not like slowly dying in human nature, we can start living our Divine Nature because that's what we really are and most of us in the Iron Age don't know it.

When we are below the line, we are only human and that is a lie.

<u>The Truth of Man, the Truth of us, is that we are Spiritual Beings in human forms.</u>

Chapter 15: You Are a Being in Human Form

There is ample evidence everywhere that mankind is in the fallen state. There are "problems" in general, which are distortions that have been made by our own actions, everywhere you look. In this state, people believe that they are intelligent but they argue with each other about many things: religion, politics, education, science, evolution, etc.

We think that it is intelligent to emphasize how people **differ** with each other. The result is a semblance of order interspersed with turmoil, chaos and distress. The turmoil is caused by our differences. We call this condition the land below the line. People who live in this land experience wars among themselves, voids and arguments, and the evidence of the absences of the true state.

Philosophically, there are some people in this land who believe that a person has a spirit or a soul which will transcend death. They have various scriptures of old to buttress their positions, There are those who believe in a heaven after death. There are those who believe that they will reincarnate over and over again until they reach the nirvana of perfection. Still others believe that this present experience of life is all that there is, and, when the death of the body occurs, there is nothing else. There is argument as to how we got here we are on Earth: evolution versus creationism. We argue over our differences.

There are a wide variety of assorted religious and scientific beliefs and people argue over their different interpretations of how to get to where they would like to go. We live in an argumentative state. Is there a state where argument does not exist!? Is there a Promised Land, a Paradise, a Heaven, a Garden of Eden, a Nirvana to be experienced? These places can not be located **physically** in the land below the line. What is the **Truth**?!

Could it be possible that there a land **above** the horizontal line and if there is, how do we get **there**. If there is, we want to know about it in our own experience while we are alive so we really want this place to be **here**. Instead of discussing all of our differences and arguing about the differences in our beliefs, is there something that all of us do have in common? Can we discuss **agreement** instead of **disagreement**? Could agreement be above the horizontal line and disagreement be below the line? The only true stating place for agreement is in the Spirit or Being that is coming to us should be allowed to come through us to produce the Golden Age.

Can we really reason together? Is there something that all the religions of the world and all the sciences can agree upon as a starting point? Well, we are all earthlings, who are alive and we all have Being, or Spirit or Life. We have Being in common and we also have human bodies, male and female, as well as human minds and hearts. We can agree that we are human beings if we place our human bodies first, or we can agree that we are Beings in human forms living on planet Earth if we give primary emphasis to Spirit. Are we only temporary human beings and nothing else, or are we Beings in human forms?

In order for people to really know the Truth of Spirit or Being, they would have to have the experience of their own spirit or Being which is not of a human form composed of materials that disintegrate at death. We know that there is a <u>human</u> component to a human being that is temporary and it **disintegrates**, but is there really a spiritual

Being within the human form that is eternal and it **integrates**?Can the presence of Being be proven while we are still alive with a human body, mind and heart that can communicate the experience to others?

Many people sincerely believe that there is life after death, the disintegration of the human form, but, once the person dies, the spirit no longer has a body to communicate the information of the survival of the spirit to us. How can we really begin to prove to ourselves that there is a spirit which transcends death? Is this an important goal!?

As long as a person functions from the standpoint of a material identity, a human identity, which is composed of a physical body with its mind and feelings, the total experience will be of a material nature. The person will have experiences known on earth by one's own mind, one's own feelings and one's own physical sensations as they relate to the material things of the earth. The total experience will be of the earth and the person will know nothing else even though a spirit or Being may be present, but unknown, to the conscious mind. A human being is earthbound, **emotionally** bound to the material earth.

We could say that human beings are trapped in a prison jail in the material land below the line. There is a door to this prison and the door is closed. The person in the jail is aware of the fact that the door is closed. They assume that the closed door is locked, **but the door is not locked.** Try the door. Open the door!

The conscious human mind is aware of the past conditions that we have recorded and read in our history books. But what is written in our history books originated through the consciousness of the writers who inhabited our fallen human state symbolized by the land below the line. The fallen human mind was not consciously aware of the invisible Being, or Spirit, which may be present, but unknown by the conscious mind.

In order for the human mind to know the Invisible Being or the Spirit, the nature of the spirit would have to be expressed through the heart, the mind and the body of a person and then, **after** the True Nature of the Spirit was expressed, the person would know by actual experience. The human mind knows what is expressed through it.

The devilish fallen mind whispers to us, "Prove to me that there is a Spirit or Being present **first**, and then, after you prove this to me, I **might** let the Being come forth through me---Maybe---but I'm not sure that I will." This is a very arrogant approach. The fallen human mind would rather rule on earth where it is a king, than serve in heaven where there is a Higher King. The devil of the human mind remains earthbound slithering in the dust like a serpent. It will not leave the material ground of the land below the line to rise up to the Land Above the Line where the Spirit that gives life to the serpent might actually dwell.

The spirit, like **air** which symbolizes it, cannot be grasped by the net of the human mind. Spirit cannot be grasped or caught like a butterfly with material nets. But the mind can experience spirit as the spirit flows through it. But Spirit, which is of finer substance than the mind, must be allowed to flow freely and unfettered through the mind. This means that the mind **must relinquish control to the indwelling spirit** and the mind, which is the king of the body in the land below the line, does not want to relinquish control to a higher power of Spirit, even if Spirit does exist.

The nature of your individual Being, which is a part of God's BEING, is not the nature of the human, mind-made experience of the fallen state. Our thesis is that if the spirit within people had been expressed constantly and consistently over the generations, there would be no fallen state; there would be a state that reflected the expression of the spirit. There would be a Spirit-made world instead of a fallen, mind made world. The only way that a person can know the reality of the spirit in expression is to let the nature of spirit express itself through one's particular equipment into the material world. This would be an interesting experiment for a maverick scientist! This would be an interesting experiment for a maverick religionist! This would be an interesting experiment for a maverick atheist!This would be an interesting experiment for a maverick agnostic! It would be an interesting experiment for any person. How about you?!

The True Nature of spirit does not contain the pollution of the earth with its faulty thinking about the importance of differences and its negative emotions. The mental offering, symbolized by the offering of Cain, is unacceptable to the LORD God, Whoever that is. There are many scientific people who state, "I know not the LORD and my mind can't prove such a God exists. I lean toward the theory of evolution".

There are many religious people who state, "I believe in my heart that there is a LORD even though I have no direct experience but I have faith that there is a God. I lean toward the scriptures, the Holy Bible, or the Koran, or the Bhagavad Gita, or the Book of Mormon, etc." But every living human being, or Being in a human form has Spirit or Life. We know we are alive and that Life is present in our own experience. Does the Reality of Life have a nature!?

We have submitted that the nature of spirit is a nature of Love, Truth and Life. If a person truly chooses to let these three Spirits of Love, Truth and Life flow through the heart, mind and body which they inhabit, then the earthly equipment will know the experience of the Spirit that they express in action on earth. The actual experience of the person who did this would be the proof. If you did this, there would be a spiritually oriented person on earth--**You**.

The problem has been that people have been so busy reacting to the problems and conditions of the material world, conditions made by fallen man, that they have little experience of radiating the nature of spirit, a nature of Love, Truth and Life, into their material world. People are material world oriented and not spiritually oriented. They have been programmed to believe that they are only human by science and religion.

The purpose of spirit in a human form is to radiate and deliver the nature of Spirit into the material world and thus bring the nature of the spiritual kingdom into the material earth. If this is done by a religious or a scientific person, the true nature of spirit, the **truth of spirit**, will be on earth where it can be known and then, the material forms generated by the spirit can be observed as spirit-filled forms.

If it is not done by a person, then the earth around that person will reveal a distortion of the power and the distortions known in the consciousness of the fallen state. Presently, we are in the land that this author chooses to describe as a land <u>below</u> the line. The expression of Spirit or Being moving through a clean consciousness would produce the material forms of <u>the land above the land</u>.

It is always possible, as long as a person is alive, to begin to radiate the nature of the spirit of Life which is present in the human body. The spirit or Being is the truth of the person. The human mind must decide to let the nature of spirit radiate through the body, mind and heart which are under its control. The human mind can decide either to let the spirit radiate, to serve the spirit into the earth, or, to continue to "do its own thing" as it has been doing since it usurped the power from Being and caused the fallen state to occur.

The attitude of the fallen human mind has been that, it would rather rule in the hell which it has produced on earth, rather than serve the spirit from the heaven into the earth. Heaven would result on earth if the spirit of God were released through the person, individually, and the people, collectively. The Law works!

The fallen human mind has created the distorted conditions of hell which are observable everywhere through a polluted consciousness. The human mind in the fallen state created books of history that reveals its actions over many generations. It documents the presence of a Brass age and an Iron age. It tells legends of a Silver and a Golden age.

It is the human mind that needs to repent before the kingdom of heaven, which is available and at hand, can be released into the earth through its inhabitants. The human mind must let the spirit come forth to prove that the spirit or Being is present. This is an individual choice. Who would be willing to do this! There is never a change that is not preceded by a willingness to change.

Many are called to let the Spirit radiate into the earth, but since so few choose to accept the invitation, then, the majority of people are not the chosen ones. The chosen ones are the ones who **choose** to let the spirit of Love, Truth and Life radiate into the earth through the human equipment. This is an **individual** choice that demonstrates love for the Intelligent Designer in this present day. The choice can not be passed on to your children, other than by your example, which may or may not influence your children to follow your example. They, too, have freedom to choose what they express.

As people go through life, they have and know the actual experience of what has been expressed through the physical forms which they inhabit. Everyone knows that they came into the world with the physical form of a newborn infant. In time, the physical form matured into the body of a toddler, then a young child, an adolescent, an adult, a middle-aged form and a mature individual. As a person with some maturity looks back in time, it is possible to realize that many tremendous changes have occurred in the different sizes and shapes of one's physical body during a lifetime.

The person has had many bodies which have changed over the years but there has been **Someone** who has been present and **Who** has not changed during all of the changes that have occurred in heart, mind and body. This Someone, this Being, <u>**YOU**</u>, have been present and remained unchangeable through all the years when the physical, mental and emotional changes took place. **YOU** have been present through all the changes which have taken place in your human body, your human mind and your human emotions. **YOU** are the ever-present, unchangeable Spirit. **YOU** are Spirit, not form. **YOU** are the True Self. **YOU** need to express your True Self on earth in order to get an earthly experience of Who You are.

It is your Being which is connected to a greater BEING that supplies the power to use the mind and the emotions. The body, mind and heart compose the material, earthly human capacities while Being, spirit, supplies the power, the design and the life which are necessary for the material form to function on earth.

The earthly capacities of the body, mind and heart of a person are filled with experiences which it has learned from interaction and association with the material forms, material thoughts and feelings that it has obtained from the material environment in which it dwells. The Being or Spirit of a person who exists at the level that is higher than the mind has knowledge and feelings from a Divine Source, the Intelligent Designer. There is an intelligent design that is coming into the earth through people, whether they are human beings or Beings in human forms, whether they dwell below the line or live above the line.

This knowledge and these feelings are inherent within the spirit and are available to be expressed through the physical body, mind and heart **if the earthly capacities will let them come forth** from inside out. The nature of Being or Spirit is a nature of total love, all truth and eternal life which is available to be released as needed, and when it is fitting, into the earth by means of the human equipment provided that the human equipment of body, mind and heart will choose to allow themselves to be used for a higher purpose, a Divine purpose. Even if the human equipment is not willing, there is some degree of creativity that enters the earth anyway. True Spirit seeps through its human creation. What seeps through is an abstraction of the True Design.

The present use of the equipment of body mind and heart is under the control of the human ego. The self-centered human ego has been interested in its own goals and ambitions. The human ego is more interested in letting "my" own self-centered will be done rather than letting "Thy" will be done. This is the point of decision. The human mind must deliberately let the spirits of Love, Truth and Life find release and expression from within one's self where they have always been available as a potential.

The conscious mind must allow the potential be actualized. Spiritual people say, Let the spirit of God out! This is a plea to the human ego, the false self, which is scheduled to pass away in due time, to repent and change. Human beings admit that they are mortal and there is ample evidence to prove this in every generation. Human forms pass away for everybody.

The world is filled with believers. Atheists believe that there is no God. Agnostics believe that there might be a God but they can't prove it. Muslims believe that Allah (the Arabic word for God) is great and Mohammed is His Prophet. The Jews believe that they are the Chosen people. Christians believe Jesus was the anointed One when he walked on earth, and in the second coming of Christ in the future. Many people who are not religious believe that they can pray to God for what they want. Buddhists believe that Siddartha Gautama was the Buddha, the enlightened One. Is there a theory about a Path that can show the Way to all people? Consider this approach to the One God.

The theory is very simple. The false-self must allow the human equipment of physical form with its mind and heart to cease its useless forays into the past and into the future by trying to change what has occurred in the past or to prevent what might occur in the future. **Past and future are states that do not exist in the present moment of reality.** The Eternal Being of an individual always dwells in the present moment of the Eternal Now.

There is only **the present moment** available to **let** the spirit of Love, Truth and Life find expression trough your heart, your mind and your body into the material circumstances of the environment. The circumstances of the immediate environment shall be used by **YOU** to determine what is fitting for YOU to release into it. Love and Truth can be used to create the divine world instead of using the inherited, polluted, "sins of the fathers" to produce physical forms that are characterized by the distorted and chaotic state below the line.

A totally new approach to the so-called problems of the world would be the conditions of the material world are not PROBLEMS!There is no need for a person to conjure up solutions to the "problems" created by the muddy waters, that symbolize the polluted content of the consciousness flowing from the sinful human heart. Instead, it would be far wiser to let the human mind and heart reveal the Spirits of Love and Truth into the immediate world around each one. As this occurs, easily and naturally, the material world must reflect your Spiritual Expression. The Law works. The Kingdom will come.

There is Good News available for you. You are not the false self which has found your experience of life so difficult to date. **You are the True Self** which resides in the Eternity of heaven which is available to be experienced on earth while you are alive to convey the experience to others.

Be your True Self. Bless your world with your presence. The way is easy and the burden is light. The world of material distortion passes away and the new heaven and the new earth finds expression because of you and your expression. Just keep doing this and the problems will disappear and the Answer shall appear in material forms. The return of the King and the return of His Golden Age as His Children re-present Him on Earth..

The person who does this faithfully will know in his or her equipment of heart, mind and body the One I Am who says:I Am the Way of Love; I Am the Truth; I Am the Life. I am not my physical form from the material world. I Am that I AM from the world of Spirit. I Am **in** this material world of form temporarily but I AM not **of** it. I Am the Spirit in this form with a heart, a mind and a body to convey My presence on Earth.

I Am alive in my personal experience in a human form on Earth. The covenant-agreement is available to be experienced. Nirvana can be achieved in this life time. A Path has been cleared for you to follow. The Door is open. Rise up my love, my fair one and come away with Me. There is a Land Above the Line where the LIGHT shines brightly. The Kingdom of Heaven is Here.

It is time for all Beings in human forms to start ***LIVING IN THE LIGHT Above The Line***! You know the Way. Will you choose to experience your Real Self by expressing your Spirit!? The Choice is yours!

What follows was my personal experience. I hope that my experience will be a visible Point of Orientation for you as you move upwards on the Path to a new and higher vision for you, a *Cosmic Vision*.

Chapter 16.: August 24, 1967
11:00 am--11:30 am

Never in my wildest imagination did I ever consider that I would actually experience the location of the Real Self and the *REAL Holy Grail*! It was Thursday 11:00 am August 24, 1967. I began to feel a little queasy as though I would be sick to my stomach. Automatically, I found myself on my knees in front of a toilet expecting to lose my breakfast, but instead of the cold, clammy feeling that accompanies nausea, I was aware of a warm, increased flow of spirit moving through my body. I was surprised that the feeling that I thought would result in illness and nausea was actually a feeling of warmness and wellness.

This flow of spirit totally enfolded me and held me on my knees in a prayerful position, and instinctively, I knew that I should not move.I "heard" a loud and authoritative voice in my consciousness from an internal source that definitely was not an external sound on my eardrums, announce the words, I AM COME THAT THE SCRIPTURES MIGHT BE FULFILLED!

I was instantly aware that the powerful and authoritative voice was no still, small voice; it was a loud and powerful voice that I instinctively knew was the voice of God. I also knew beyond belief that from my position as a point of life that originated in God, that in order for me to reach the radiance from God, I had to rise up from my focus of the Spirit of Life through the Spirit of Truth and through the Spirit of Love to reach the true point of Origin of the radiance that comes to me from the Higher Level of the LORD God, or the LORD of Lords.

I also knew that the Spirits of Life, Truth and Love are connected to each other as a braided cord that could not be separated from each other because they are One Spirit. (This information would prove invaluable to me much later when I began writing, but at this awesome moment of time, I had no idea of writing anything.)

I was certain of one basic condition: The Spirit of the invisible LORD can be exemplified on earth through a person; The spirit of Love on earth can be exemplified by a person; The Spirit of Truth on earth can be exemplified by a person; and the Spirit of Life on earth can be exemplified by a person. This knowledge that the **invisible** spirits of God can be personified through **visible** people would later prove to be an invaluable key to understanding the allegorical nature of the many scriptures of the world.

As the Spirit flowed through me with increasing intensity, all of the experiences of my life on earth flashed rapidly through my conscious awareness in great detail with the understanding that the Spirit of God had indeed been with me through all of these experiences. The rapidity and the speed of the review of the images in my consciousness produced what I can only describe as a complete and thorough but understandable blur of events. This was a total loving, factual and accurate review--with no condemnation--of everything that I had ever done in my experience of life on earth as the events flashed through my consciousness.

I was impressed by the speed of the review, by the "rapid downloading" of all of my actions and the totality of everything. The speed of the review carried the atmosphere of loving, forgiving, great patience and understanding.I was surprised that I did not experience any fear. (Later, I thought that it was consoling to me that God not only cares about me and knows all these details of my personal behavior, but also He is aware of the behaviors of billions of others who are on this planet in their human nature conditions and behaviors.)

I viewed everything that I was allowed to see from my experiences of life on earth from a detached, objective standpoint that I can only describe as a location for me in "the timelessness of time" which is above the world of material form. Time had indeed seemed to stand still. I was One-with my Creator in the presence of my Creator in a dimension never before experienced by me.

I was aware that during this review, that I had always been totally enfolded in the warmth of God's love in this temporary sojourn on earth and, more importantly, as a result of this experience, I knew, not just believed, but really knew that there is no death for God's children. From that moment on, the fear of death was gone from my experience because there is no such thing as death for spiritual beings. We are either Spirits in physical human forms or Spirits Who are not in physical forms. But, in forms or not, we are spiritual beings in human forms while we are on earth and we shall continue to live when our physical bodies are no longer needed by us as vehicles to be used during our time on earth.

I was keenly aware that I was a spiritual being and that I was and I am a member of the body of God in heaven and on earth. I was also aware that almost everyone else on earth is not aware of their spiritual nature and that all spiritual beings in human forms are members of the body of God who are not aware of Who they really are. I was aware that they should be aware of who they are but that they do not know their true nature or know their purpose; and that this is not the fault of God Who is with everyone always.

I was aware that I had been born into a world of the spirit and in this new identity, I would be a co-creator with God while on earth in a human form and that I must use the spirit of God to create the material forms on earth that are created by me; otherwise the mess, the chaos and the terrible distortions are the creation of mankind in its separation from the consciousness of God. The exact nature of the earthly creation would be determined by me as it unfolds in the earthly moments of my creative activity. God would not tell "me" what to do but I was aware that what I would do in His Spirit would be harmonious with the work of other spirits in human forms who use His Spirit to create the conditions in which we must live on earth.

During this amazing experience, there was **no fear** of God; there was only an intense state **of awe and appreciation** for the intense flow of love in which I was enfolded and which all other beings in human forms are also enfolded whether they know it or not. I was surprised that there was no negative fear in this fantastic experience; only love and the flowing warmth of love in action on earth.

I **knew** that I must use the Spirit of Truth and the Spirit of Love that radiate from God to produce forms of Life on earth as long as I am here in a physical form. I knew that I would "return" to God when I was no longer in an earthly form because I was and I am a part of God always. I was aware that heaven and earth are One for spiritual beings.

The only separation between my Being with its human form and God was in **my** human consciousness. In this new state of Cosmic Consciousness, we are One Spirit. Of course, I was not the totality of Almighty God, but I Am a part of His Spirit as a small spiritual rock is a small part of a mountain of Spirit. My mission and the mission of all God-beings sent into the earth by God is to extend the blessings of God from Heaven, the place where God dwells, to earth and to bring the design of His Kingdom here on earth through us exactly where we are into the earthly circumstances where we are.

As the ecstasy of this intense experience faded away, I noticed that a half an hour of earthly time had passed. I was "returned" to my earthly focus of self once more (I knew that I hadn't gone anywhere physically) with a conscious awareness of my True Identity. I am an individual aspect, a Spirit of God, Who belongs to God.

My main thought, which will never leave me, would be the substance of the teaching of the two great commandments: "How shall I express the Spirit of Almighty God into the Earth through my human capacities!?" and "How shall I help my fellow men and women to know Who they are and why they are here!?" The choice of creative service would be mine and God would not tell me how to do it. He trusts me to re-present Him!

The longing of my heart would be to find a way to let the people of the world, who are existing in a fallen state of human consciousness, come to know why we are here. How can I help my fellow Spirits to remember and to experience Who they really are and Why we are here? One thing I knew for certain in my new personal awareness: the Spirit of God is moving through all of His Children on earth and We are One with Him in Spirit.

The problem is that our individual hearts, minds and bodies are not revealing the Holy Grail that they were designed to be. The answer is within us and not in the material world. I stood up and walked into my material world with a new consciousness of the Spirit that I Am. It was 11:30 am, Thursday, August 24, 1967.

I am a different person. I am in a state of euphoria! I am aware that the conditions of world are a terrible distortion of the heavenly design. Somebody must do something about it. I know that I have accepted the responsibility to do something about it. I don't know how I will do it. The path will have to unfold as I walk in the Spirit of being born again into the world of Spirit.

My fellow human beings, my fellow Spiritual Beings in human male and female forms, need to know Who they are!. Of one thing I am certain! No matter what earthly pressure comes from my environment, nothing will stand in the way of my determination to express the Spirit of God into the world of form. I had no idea of what I would do next or how I would do it.

Author's Note: This amazing event in my life was a one-time occurrence. This intense flow of the spirit has never occurred again since August 24, 1967 even though there were many times that I hoped that it would re-occur and that many times I prayed for information and guidance. Much later, there were many instances in my writing when I would feel "warm" chills run down my spine, or hairs "raise" on the back of my neck when something particularly important or revealing came into written form through me.

I have always considered August 24, 1967 as the day of my first death, the death of the human ego self consciousness which passed away. It is also the date of my birth into the realm of knowing my Spirit, the elevation to Cosmic Consciousness, the date when I was "born again" of the Spirit. I had the knowledge that the REAL Holy Grail was indeed within a person and not external to oneself.

I was aware that the flowing Spirit from the Father, the radiance from God, was moving through my human capacities. I was aware that this is the Truth for all of us. I had unknowingly tuned into God's channel that He radiates through His Creation. I know the radiation is there in my personal experience of it. My heart longs to be in the Spirit of His radiation. This is the primary longing of my heart which is over and above everything in the material world which I now view as atoms and molecules that clothe the Spirit.

One thing for sure, I was certain that my experience of Life on earth would change because I was a "new and different" person as a result of this awesome experience on August 24, 1967 between 11:00 and 11:30 am when I was positioned on my knees with my head bowed, unable and unwilling to raise my head, and immoveable in communion, a common union, with my Creator. Where would this fantastic experience lead me as I finally stood up and walked into the sunlight with the warm glow of euphoria lingering in my memory as I felt thoroughly examined, naked, unashamed and accepted? Where will this incident lead me? Where do I go from here!?

As times goes on, will I understand more in the days to come?

Chapter 17: Born Again

Now I really know, in the reality of my living experience, the meaning of the term, "Born again." I know the experience of being born into the world of Spirit from my former world of material identity for 40 years, (since I would be 41 on my next birthday.) I know what it means to **know** that I am an individual aspect of God and that this is my True Identity which survives the material flesh body with its human mind and the wide range of human emotions. I am a piece of God in action on earth through these human capacities. I understand the phrase that God is Everywhere.

The human capacities are the means on earth for me to express my Spiritual Self, the One I Am. This is an awesome, unforgettable, humbling, and at the same time, an elevating experience that could be and should be a common human experience. I also knew that I could not prove that this internal experience happened! As I became aware of my divine eternal nature, my thoughts turned to the healing powers that I had heard as a youth from biblical stories: the magical powers of Moses; the healing of the sick and the deformed by Jesus; the strength of a Samson.; the courage of David. Did I have any of these supernatural physical powers?!

In my euphoric state, I tried many different ways to use my new spiritual awareness. Can I touch someone and heal them instantaneously? Could I blink my eyes and cure a partially blind friend? Could I cause water to part? Could I walk on water? I tried these things as carefully as I could. **Nothing that I attempted worked!** I was bound by the scientific laws that govern life on earth. I had no new and unusual powers.

After some initial experimentation, I quickly discovered that I remained bound and subject to the way that things function on earth and that the existing physical laws of the planet were not transcended in my own experience as a result of my new awareness. I quickly concluded that I had no supernatural powers over the world of time and matter. The laws of Cause and Effect, gravity, physics and chemistry continued to operate as they had before my internal enlightening experience. The only change that I experienced was a change in consciousness that there is a Divine Source, God Almighty, and that I am a part, an offspring, of this Great Spirit.

I really felt as a "newborn" in the world of spirit. I was seeing the world of my environment from a higher perspective, higher than my former **material** perspective, because now I was able to view all material things as containing the spirit and presence of God, while before I was aware only of the atoms and molecules of material things without the binding spiritual component of the Creator of the Universe. I reasoned that if this Spirit is in me, then it must be in all people and things. The Spirit is in all forms. The Spirit does not impose itself in the physical forms; the Spirit just **is** within the physical forms, as man in his present fallen state has created the forms.

The Spirit is a state of **Being**, not a state of **becoming**. Spirit doesn't change. I know what the meaning of "**is**" is! The Spirit **is!** This Spirit is everywhere and there are pockets of matter throughout the universe contained and enfolded in this living spirit of God and one of these forms of matter is called planet Earth by us. The Spirit is in the planet and the Spirit is in the inhabitants of the planet.

Much later, I began to see that the many forms which I was observing on earth were distortions or imperfect creations of a True Design, and that ALL the distortions of the Divine Design were introduced at the earthly level of man. The True Design is in the Spirit; the distortions of the True design are introduced by man in his fallen state. After being "born again" by my one-time spiritual experience, I had to learn to walk slowly and carefully in the spirit, before I could run.

When I did try to run too fast, I fell. I saw things differently than I had ever seen before and I had to control my impulses to try to tell the world of my new vision. My heart wanted to shout the good news from the housetops, but my mind cautioned that most people will never believe something that they themselves have never experienced.

There were many times that I tried "shouting from the housetops to try to force someone to see", but it never worked. If they couldn't see what I was talking about, I had no power to force my view upon anyone. Their vision remained the same material vision that they had with the exception that some people were able to learn a little more from my view of things. Unsuccessfully, I tried to use undue pressure and emotions to **try** to force others to "understand" as I saw the material world which I was observing from a higher perspective.

I learned quickly that you cannot force a person to see. But, in my enthusiasm and stupidity, I tried and I failed. Slowly, I learned that I must let the light of understanding shine on the material path that others were walking instead of shining the light of my spiritual "brilliance" into their eyes, which only blinded them more than they could see normally before I tried to help them.

My initial efforts did not help my friends and family; my misguided, enthusiastic efforts actually hurt and confused the very people that I was trying to help. My efforts to try to help them seemed to release negative emotions from them of anger and resentment. No one can be forced to "see", to perceive their worlds as they really are, because people see their worlds through their own state of consciousness, which is in varying degrees of pollution.

There is a **spiritual** state of consciousness and there is a **material** state of consciousness. The main difference is the experience of spiritual identity imparts a higher vision than the more familiar material viewpoint. If the condition of human consciousness is clouded, the people will see things darkly until the condition of their consciousness is cleared by the experience of spiritual identity. I understood that Spiritual things are Spiritually discerned from the higher level of spirit. The level of Spirit is higher than the level of form. Eventually, I learned to walk more slowly and to act more carefully in my relationships with others.

In my personal experience, I did not know anyone who had experienced what I have described this far. If others had the experience, they didn't talk about it to me. I needed to learn if there were other people who may have experienced this change in consciousness.

I also thought for a moment, from my medical background, that I might have had an hallucination or a schizophrenic episode. I dismissed this thought rather quickly, but I reconsidered it on regular basis for a while..

What happened within me did not seem like an illness; it seemed like health and wellness. For the time being, I decided to remain alert in the present, bask in the glow of the unusual, awesome experience and remain quiet while I tried to figure out what happened to me. Of course, I was shocked by the unexpected nature of the experience but I did not doubt it at all. I was amazed that the Spiritual Experience was not common knowledge and promoted by religions and science.

What will happen next!? It didn't seem important as I enjoyed the wonder and knowledge of my experience. Where do I go from here!? I don't know but I would patiently let whatever unfold in due course. What I needed to know came into my hands in the form of a book written by a medical doctor many years ago at the turn of the last century. His work was a comfort to me.

Chapter 18: Cosmic Consciousness

Some time later, after my awesome, personal experience into a spiritual state of consciousness, I was fortunate to become aware of a book, entitled, **Cosmic Consciousness,** originally written by Richard Maurice Bucke, M.D. in 1900 and later re-published by Causeway Books in 1974. This book described the shift from the state of self consciousness to a new state which he called, *Cosmic Consciousness*. Dr. Bucke's presentation and his knowledge of the shift in consciousness that he had experienced validated my own experience of being "born again".

Dr. Bucke beautifully describes the mark of the Cosmic Sense in individuals who have had the experience as follows:

a. The subjective light.
b. The moral elevation
c. The intellectual illumination.
d. The sense of immortality
e. The loss of the fear of death
f. The loss of the sense of sin.
g. The suddenness, instantaneousness of the awakening.
h. The previous character of the man- intellectual, moral and physical.
i. The Age of the illumination.
j. The added charm to the personality so that men and women are always(?) strongly attracted to the person.

k. The transfiguration of the subject of the change as seen by others when the cosmic sense is actually present.

Dr. Bucke continues: "It must not be supposed that because a man has cosmic consciousness he is therefore omniscient or infallible. The greatest of these men are in a sense in the position, though on a higher plane, of children who have just become self conscious. These men have just reached a new phase of consciousness—they have not yet had time nor the opportunity to master this new experience **(This was important to me!).** True, they have reached a higher mental level; but on that level there can and will be comparative wisdom and comparative foolishness just as there is on the level of simple or self consciousness".

(Personally, it was good for me to read and to become aware that other people had a similar experience to the one which I had encountered. As I previously said, I did have thoughts that I may have been hallucinating or that I may have been mentally ill. I hesitated talking to anyone about my 30 minute spiritual experience. (I had heard that people who had an experience of God were locked up in an institution.)

Dr. Bucke also listed the names of people whom he believed had experienced the shift from self consciousness to cosmic consciousness. The impressive list of 43 names includes Moses the Deliverer, Gideon, Isaiah, Gautama the Buddha, Socrates, Jesus the Christ, the Apostle Paul, Roger Bacon, Dante, Francis Bacon, Walt Whitman and most importantly, many others of his contemporaries who represent the common ordinary man, and one woman.

His book details the experiences of Cosmic Consciousness for these people in greater detail. The good news for me was that the actual experience of Cosmic Consciousness had been experienced by others and that it is available to be experienced by others. My desire was that the shift in consciousness which I had encountered in my personal experience, should be extended to as many others as possible and I would work to achieve this goal to helping others. This change in consciousness seemed beneficial to humanity and, in my professional career, I worked, and believed the motto of health care, **In Service to Humanity**. (I was also reminded of the impressive message above the stage in my Junior High School auditorium: **Enter To Learn, Go Forth To Serve.)**

During the past 37 years, I have been privileged to write the symbolic interpretations of the words and works of people, whom I label as **The Stars of the Scriptures.** My intention was to make their new state of consciousness available to all those who are willing to make the journey from a fallen state of human nature to Man made in the image and likeness of God, a journey from below the line to a journey above the line.

In the process of writing, I slowly and gradually came to understand over many years *The Challenge of Moses*, *The Songs and Wisdom of David and Solomon*, *The Mission of Jesus and John*, *The Testimony of the Major Prophets*, *The Recitations of Mohammed*, *The Leadership of Joseph Smith*, **The Scriptures from the Orient**, *The Truth of Nanak and the Sikhs* and some insights from my personal experiences, which I call, *The Spirit Is in the Form, The REAL Holy Grail* and *LIVING IN THE LIGHT Above The Line.*

These books were written to introduce the people of the world, in both the religious and the scientific communities, to the experience of personal enlightenment, Cosmic Consciousness, Unity Consciousness, Christ Consciousness, The Ark of the Covenant, the Shekinah, the Covenant Agreement, the Kingdom of Heaven, Nirvana, the Tao, the Oneness with the Father and finding *The Holy Grail* within oneself.

All of these phrases are, in my mind, the same thing. All of these names refer to the shift in consciousness from self consciousness to cosmic consciousness, which is necessary for Man to return to the ascended position from which he fell, which is called "the fall of man". If you accept the false premise of "I'm only human you know" and continue to express the nature of the false self, you will never experience who you really are in the cosmic sense.

The challenge of living on earth is to return to Who you really are while you are on earth in a human form so that you can speak of your experience to others: A child of God, an angel of the Lord in human form, a Blessed One, a Spirit who temporarily inhabits a human form.

It is impossible to know your True Self unless you begin with the correct premise that there is a True Identity. You must express your True Self to know who you are, otherwise your experience will continue to be the experience of the false self. This book has been written for those who want to know the Truth of their own Beings on this side of the grave while they can be active co-creators with God on earth by using His Spirit in the Creative Process.

Of course, there are those people who are unwilling to change or who don't want to think about changing. Their attitude is "Prove to me (their minds which are in a fallen state) that there is such an experience of the True Self and then, after you have proven it to me to my satisfaction, then, I might be willing to change!"No change ever occurs in anyone unless it is preceded by a **willingness** to change. The Law of Sowing and Reaping is in constant operation and it is never repealed.

If you express your present state of self consciousness, you shall surely reap the results of that state of consciousness. Or, if you express the nature of the Cosmic Self, you shall surely reap the nature of this Higher Self, your True Eternal Self, which will reveal to your own heart, mind and body the actual experience of the Divine Self, the Spirit Who you really are.

A horizontal line has been drawn on earth and this line of demarcation has always been here since the fall of Man. This horizontal line is seen as a line of **separation** between the human self and the Divine Self. However, this line of separation is also a line of **connection**.

Below this horizontal line dwell the citizens of the world who are trapped in their human nature state of existence.

Above the horizontal line are those who have experienced the Truth of their Divine, Cosmic Nature. The area above the line, which is the dwelling place of the True Identity of Man, is and has always been only one step away from your present state of consciousness which is very familiar to you. It is not a physical step, it is a step into Cosmic Consciousness, into Nirvana, into the Kingdom of Heaven which is at hand, into Enlightenment, into the Tao.

The earthly experience, seemingly the only experience possible on earth, can be visualized below this horizontal line. It is the only experience known by the people in this familiar state. This fallen state of human nature can be described as a confused state of existence, a state of dying, a slow journey from birth to death until the finality of death occurs with the hope that there might be something more.

This state described as below the horizontal line is not the living experience designed by God for His Children. It is a dying state known by people on earth for many generations since the fall of mankind. There is another state to be experienced that does not lead to death. The new experience leads to new life. Are you really willing to stop dying and start living by entering the new state!? The new state is "new" to people who are trapped in the fallen human nature state.

The new state is not unknown to God. The new state is the True State from which man "fell", the Garden of Eden state, and, by reason of the fall, mankind lost consciousness of the original state which is characterized by Life, not death. There is no such thing as "dead" Life. The nature of Life is to be what it is--**Alive**! The nature of Life is to be alive! Life cannot die.

The Reality of Life, the Spirit of Life, is eternal, not temporal. "Dead" Life is a contradiction in terms. The nature of the substance above the horizontal line is living substance, invisible, living, spiritual substance that is eternal in nature. This living substance of the Spirit of Life has been written about and spoken about in the various scriptures of the world.

The scriptures were written by men who had experienced a new state of consciousness within their own experience. They wrote their messages in the scriptures to share their experience of Spiritual Consciousness with others. The purpose of the Holy Scriptures is to lead people to God.

Consider this premise: If man's state of consciousness **fell** while he was living on earth, why can't his consciousness **rise** while he is living on the same earth?! Perhaps this is the hidden message in the scriptures!

Can Cosmic Consciousness unearth the message in the Scriptures and find the missing Holy Grail?!

Let's begin and continue the personal journey for you to discover the Truth, the Truth of your own Being. A line has been drawn on earth which is a line of **connection** and not a line of **separation**. This line of connection has point of opening in it for you to pass through.

May you choose to begin
LIVING IN THE LIGHT Above The Line.
I Am with you in the Way.
• *You have received An Invitation to Cosmic Consciousness*

Anthony John Monaco © August 27, 2005

Epilogue

I have never considered myself to be a poet. Here are two poems which are the only two poems that I have written.They are offered to you as an example of what can happen spontaneously if you go with the flow of the Spirit within. The words flowed automatically and spontaneously from my pen many years ago as I was moved by the Spirit. I have never changed or rearranged a word.

This first poem is a call to maturity. There is no condemnation for being in the fallen state but there is a call to recognize our present predicament. I used to think that the term, Children of Men, was a compliment. Now, I see the term as men and women who have not matured spiritually and who act as children rather than the Spiritually mature men and women that we should be, and that we are in Spirit.

The Children Of Men

Oh Earth and its inhabitants
Must you persist in Fallen Ways
As though there were no precedents
That led us to these troubled days.

How can strife cease for humankind
Unless the change begins with one
How futile it is to blame the whole
For tangled webs we all have spun.

Untangle self from circumstance,
From world materiality.
Experience a new found state
Where those who serve are truly free.

<u>Children of men, won't you mature</u>
And waken to your True Design
Fulfillment lies in what you give
Each moment sown in space and time.

There is no need to search for Peace
You are the goal for which you seek
Express your spark and light the world!
Earth's inherited by the meek.

Anthony John Monaco   Memorial Day 1973

This second poem is a declaration of an individual person who has recognized the responsibility of accepting the **call to maturity** and what needs to be done to function from this new and higher level of consciousness. It is an invitation to others to join in the magnification of the Light of Truth on earth so that the world will change to reveal the presence of the LIGHT that comes from Center. All of us are Centers of Light.

I Am A Center

**I am a Center at work in the field.
Alone I stand and serve, I stand alone.
I am not to be a burden but a blessing.
My Center exists to bless the earth.**

**I am a part of a larger spiritual Center.
It is unseen in form but it exists in spirit.
I am connected in spirit to this Center.
I am divided in form so I might have freedom
of movement in the world of form.
My burden is light because it is a spiritual connection.
All connections in form are burdensome.**

**It is not necessary for Center to grow.
The true center is everywhere, complete, whole.
The nature of center needs to be expressed into form.
I am interested in expressing into form what exists in Center
and is missing in form.
That is why I came into the earth.**

**Center is everywhere.
As I express my Center, the Center in all things
rise up to meet me and I them.
In true Centering, we are all One.
Only form separates us.
Look beyond the form and see me as I Am.
As I Am, so are you, we are One.**

Matter is a veil that divides us;
the division is only in the material mind.
We are here to bless this earth, this dust.
I welcome other Centers at work in the field.
Together we are the Revelation of Center.
We bring light into the darkness of this world.

I Am the light of the world.
My form bears witness to the Light.
In false identity I believed that I was not the Light.
but only bore witness to the light of another.

You are the light of the world, too.
We are One--you and I and they.
The Lord our God is One; each One is God.
This is the Truth for all.
For God excludes no one.

My light shines to draw forth your light.
Let your light so shine that you may know me.
As I know you.
For we are One, we have always been One.
We shall always be One.

Our kingdom is not of this material world.
We are here to bless this world.
So that our world will be here.
Let us be about our Father's business.
The restoration of this earth.

Let us make man in our image, after our likeness.
This was the word of God, it is the word of God.
The breath of life is breathed into man.
And he became a living soul.

Anthony John Monaco   **May 9, 1975**

●

Here is a dot symbol of your Center.
●
Let the Spirit of God that is coming directly <u>to</u> you come <u>through</u> you.
●
My Spirit Is With You In The Way.

●

LIVING IN THE LIGHT
Above The Line

_____

(In a World of Turmoil)

About the Author

Anthony John Monaco, a retired health care professional after 50 years of service to sick people, has been interested in the cause of disease at the physical, mental and emotional levels of individuals. His scientific background and inquiring mind led him to consider spiritual approaches to health.

He has written extensively on the divinely inspired, specific authors whose teachings were directly responsible for the major religions of mankind. It is obvious that their teachings have not been followed to produce the harmony of the Divine Kingdom.

His latest book presents a simplified, logical and scientific way to Cosmic Consciousness. The Path leads to the revelation of the actual experience of your True Self as an eternal Spiritual Being that resides in your temporary human form while you are on Earth. You can discover your purpose to re-present the Spirit of the Intelligent Designer exactly where you are as you participate in the creative process to create a heavenly environment for posterity.

He explains how the individual and collective behaviors of people have created the turmoil and chaos of human nature in accordance with the Law of Cause and Effect over many generations of time. By the intelligent use of the same Law, individual and collective Spiritual Expression can also create the True Design from the Intelligent Designer for planet Earth. The Author invites you to become aware of the Path to Cosmic Consciousness.